Student Life in Catholic Higher Education:
Advancing Good Practice

CreateSpace Independent Publishing Platform
ISBN-13: 978-1545315897
ISBN-10: 1545315892

Association of Catholic Colleges and Universities (ACCU)
One Dupont Circle NW
Suite 650
Washington, DC 20036
http://www.accunet.org

Table of Contents

PREFACE *Michael Galligan-Stierle*   7
Association of Catholic Colleges and Universities

SECTION ONE: **PRESIDENTIAL REFLECTIONS**   9

CHAPTER 1 From Student Affairs to the Presidency: 11
Leadership as a Vocation (One President's Story)
Donna M. Carroll, Dominican University

CHAPTER 2 Student Affairs: The Beating Heart of the Academy   15
Bassam M. Deeb, Trocaire College

CHAPTER 3 Providing Formation and Enabling the 'Authentic Self':   21
The Work of Student Affairs
John J. De Gioia, Georgetown University

CHAPTER 4 Pope Francis: A Model of Leadership and   27
Management at Catholic Institutions and a
Guide for Senior Student Affairs Officers
Rev. James J. Maher, CM, Niagara University

CHAPTER 5 Job or Vocation: The Transformation of a   33
Student Affairs Professional
Robert A. Pastoor, Saint Joseph's College

CHAPTER 6 The Roles of Residence Hall Staff Members   37
in the Mission of the Catholic University
Rev. Mark L. Poorman, CSC, University of Portland

CHAPTER 7 Fostering Transformation through Both   41
the Unexpected and the Mundane
Mark C. Reed, Saint Joseph's University

SECTION TWO: **TODAY'S LANDSCAPE**   45

CHAPTER 8 Setting the Stage: Results of a Survey of   47
Senior Student Affairs Officers
Sandra M. Estanek, Canisius College

CHAPTER 9 Getting Connected: Institutes, Organizations,   53
and Opportunities
*Alexandra Weber Bradley, Association of
Catholic Colleges and Universities*

SECTION THREE: **THEORETICAL PERSPECTIVES**   59

CHAPTER 10   The Living Tradition of *Ex corde Ecclesiae*   61
or Student Affairs

Barbara Humphrey McCrabb, United States
Conference of Catholic Bishops

CHAPTER 11   A Christian Anthropology for Student Development   65

Michael J. James, Boston College

CHAPTER 12   Character Formation and Moral Development: 69
Creating an Intentional Framework

Catherine WoodBrooks, Assumption College

SECTION FOUR: **PRACTICAL APPLICATIONS**   75

PRINCIPLE ONE: Welcomes all students into a vibrant community
that celebrates God's love for all.

CHAPTER 13   Catholic Hospitality: The Foundation for   79
Community in Catholic Higher Education

Lisa L. Kirkpatrick, St. Edward's University

CHAPTER 14   Faith Matters: Supporting Students'   83
Religious Diversity

Kristine Cyr Goodwin, Providence College

CHAPTER 15   Race and Social Justice: Lessons from Ferguson   89
and St. Louis University

Mona Hicks and Kent Porterfield, Saint Louis University

CHAPTER 16   Walking the Two-Way Bridge: Transgender at Catholic   95
Colleges and Universities

Sandra M. Estanek, Canisius College

PRINCIPLE TWO: Grounds policies, practices, and decisions in the
teachings and living tradition of the Church. Builds and prepares the
student affairs staff to make informed contributions to the Catholic
mission of the institution.

CHAPTER 17   Developing a Catholic Culture: Catholic   103
Cultural Competency as a Critical Skill

Josh A. Hengemuhle, University of St. Thomas (MN)

CHAPTER 18   Making Mission Matter: Recruitment and   109
Supervision of Mission

John Felio and Jabrina Robinson, Siena College

CHAPTER 19 Onboarding for Mission   **113**
Jennifer Mussi Nolan, Fordham University

CHAPTER 20 Assessing the Impact of Student Affairs on Mission   **117**
Erin R. Ebersole, Immaculata University

PRINCIPLE THREE: Enriches student integration of faith and reason through provision of co-curricular learning opportunities.

CHAPTER 21 Genuine Collaboration Between Student Affairs and Academic Affairs   **123**
Terri L. Mangione and Margaret Cain McCarthy, Canisius College

CHAPTER 22 The Changing Role of the Athletic Director   **129**
Jay DeFruscio, Atlantic 10 Conference

CHAPTER 23 Working with Controversial Speakers and Events on a Catholic Campus   **133**
Todd A. Olson, Georgetown University

PRINCIPLE FOUR: Creates opportunities for students to experience, reflect upon, and act from a commitment to justice, mercy, and compassion, and in light of Catholic social teaching to develop respect and responsibility for all, especially those most in need.

CHAPTER 24 Educating for Justice and Compassion: Catholic Social Teaching and the Work of Student Affairs   **139**
Thomas Mogan, Boston College

CHAPTER 25 *Laudato Si* and Its Relevance for Student Affairs   **145**
Rev. Dennis E. Tamburello, OFM, Siena College

PRINCIPLE FIVE: Challenges students to high standards of personal behavior and responsibility through the formation of character and virtues.

CHAPTER 26 College Student Discipline and Catholic Identity   **151**
Andrew Skotnicki, Manhattan College
Colette McCarrick Geary, College of St. Scholastica

CHAPTER 27 Sexual Misconduct: Title IX and Catholic Mission   **157**
Kathleen J. Byrnes, Villanova University

CHAPTER 28 Threat Assessment, Risk Management, and Catholic Mission   **161**
Marisa R. Randazzo, Georgetown University

PRINCIPLE SIX: Invites and accompanies students into the life of the Catholic Church through prayer, liturgy, sacraments, and spiritual direction.

CHAPTER 29   Richly, Deeply Supporting the Spiritual   **169**
Development of All
Julie Donovan Massey, St. Norbert College

CHAPTER 30   The Death of a Student: Lessons from a   **173**
Catholic Campus
Rev. Jay Fostner, OPraem, St. Norbert College

PRINCIPLE SEVEN: Seeks dialogue among religious traditions and with contemporary culture to clarify beliefs and to foster mutual understanding in the midst of tensions and ambiguities.

CHAPTER 31   Creating an Interfaith Culture at a Catholic   **179**
University and Meeting the Spiritual and
Religious Needs of All Students
*Lisa R. Reiter, Loyola University Chicago and
Crystal Caruana Sullivan, University of Dayton*

CHAPTER 32   Praying Together: Celebrating Ritual in   **185**
Inclusive Communities
Michael Lovette-Colyer, University of San Diego

PRINCIPLE EIGHT: Assists students in discerning and responding to their vocations, understanding potential professional contributions, and choosing particular career directions.

CHAPTER 33   Mission-centric Recruitment   **191**
Edward P. Wright, Mount St. Mary's University

CHAPTER 34   The Manresa Program: Learning, Meaning,   **197**
Calling, and Career
Deborah Cady Melzer, Le Moyne College

Preface

As anyone familiar with the higher education enterprise knows, student learning takes place both inside and outside the classroom. At a Catholic institution, student life is especially distinct, as programs and services seek to develop students spiritually, socially, emotionally, and intellectually in the context of Catholic identity and university mission. As a result, student life professionals play a critical role in student learning, whether it is in the residence halls or recreation centers, within student government or freshmen orientation, introducing a speaker series or engaging in a career counseling session, leading a disciplinary hearing or heading a service trip.

Student affairs professionals who serve at Catholic institutions have long recognized this special role, but for many years, were without resources to help them navigate their distinctive situation. Then, in 2002, Sandra M. Estanek edited *Understanding Student Affairs at Catholic Colleges and Universities: A Comprehensive Resource.* The book was the first of its kind to focus on student affairs in Catholic higher education and the unique role that lay staff and faculty perform to provide this vital service at Catholic colleges and universities.

In the years since that book's publication, many seminars and conferences have been held and research undertaken on the structure and demographics of student affairs in Catholic higher education. That learning has led to the creation of this book. Working closely with the Association for Student Affairs at Catholic Colleges and Universities and the Jesuit Association of Student Personnel Administrators, the Association of Catholic Colleges and Universities asked 25 of the best and brightest practitioners to share their wisdom and best practices to assist their colleagues. Because the research showed that more Catholic college and university presidents have risen from a position within student affairs into the presidency than ever before, we also asked eight sitting presidents to share their experience of rising from within student affairs and offer advice to those in the field. Using the structure and insights of the *Principles of Good Practice for Student Affairs at Catholic Colleges and Universities* (2010), the four editors of this book asked writers to incorporate their student affairs experiences with the content of the principles, as well as the seminal work for Catholic universities, *Ex corde Ecclesiae.*

This book is designed to be a foundational text for practitioners, examining what it means to integrate Catholic identity and university mission into the work of student affairs professionals. The inclusion of theoretical, reflective, and practical perspectives is intentional, as we envision that the book will be used for professional development activities and graduate preparation programs.

In addition — and more importantly — the editors committed to include here some of the most challenging issues of our sector, from student activism to working with transgender students to navigating controversial events on campus. We hope that this book, with its willingness to engage the issues of our day, offers insights on how you might be able to be the compassionate presence of Christ on your campus, whether at the margins or engaged in the ordinary business of student learning.

On behalf of the editors, I am grateful to the contributors who provide practical guidance and personal reflections on student life in Catholic higher education. Without their willingness to reflect on their journey and share their learnings, this book would not have come into existence. Their writings give testimony to the significant role student affairs professionals play in the lives of students every day. Thank you for all you do for Catholic higher education and the student lives that are changed forever because of your dedication to and love for your profession.

— Michael Galligan-Stierle, Ph.D.

SECTION ONE

Presidential Reflections

CHAPTER 1   From Student Affairs to the Presidency: **11**
Leadership as a Vocation
(One President's Story)
Donna M. Carroll, Dominican University

CHAPTER 2   Student Affairs: The Beating Heart   **15**
of the Academy
Bassam M. Deeb, Trocaire College

CHAPTER 3   Providing Formation and Enabling   **21**
the 'Authentic Self': The Work of
Student Affairs
John J. De Gioia, Georgetown University

CHAPTER 4   Pope Francis: A Model of Leadership and   **27**
Management at Catholic Institutions and
a Guide for Senior Student Affairs Officers
Rev. James J. Maher, CM, Niagara University

CHAPTER 5   Job or Vocation: The Transformation of   **33**
a Student Affairs Professional
Robert A. Pastoor, Saint Joseph's College

CHAPTER 6   The Roles of Residence Hall Staff Members   **37**
in the Mission of the Catholic University
*Rev. Mark L. Poorman, CSC, University of
Portland*

CHAPTER 7   Fostering Transformation through Both   **41**
the Unexpected and the Mundane
Mark C. Reed, Saint Joseph's University

CHAPTER 1

From Student Affairs to the Presidency: Leadership as Vocation (One President's Story)

Donna M. Carroll

I always have had a ferocious appetite for responsibility. Early in my student affairs career I used to adopt homeless tasks, a project here, a committee assignment there. In hindsight, it was less about building a portfolio and more about knocking down obstacles to student development. I moved from dean of students to college dean, and then one day the president called me into her office and said, "You are going to be my next vice president for advancement. Just think of yourself as a dean of students for alumnae/i!" *And I still do.*

There is no doubt that I have a particular way of inhabiting the role of president because I began my career in student affairs. At the same time, the president that I am is not just a matter of origin; rather, it has a lot to do with the mission of the Catholic, Dominican university that I lead and the fit between the two, refined by two decades of experience. Here is a bit of my *vocation* story.

STUDENT AFFAIRS BEGINNINGS

I am thankful every day that I studied higher education, and that my doctorate is in counseling, with a concentration in student personnel administration. Those were nontraditional degrees for a president 20-plus years ago, but Rosary College was looking for something different in its first lay president and the search committee took a risk on discipline for the sake of disposition and experience.

From the beginning, I had a sense of the university not only as an enterprise, but also as a community, and that relationship-centered approach still defines my leadership style. It allowed me to recognize quickly that tenure is a blood tie and that the dynamics among faculty are often acutely personal, as in a family. When we changed the name of the college to Dominican University in 1997, I donned my dean's hat and travelled the country answering questions and drying tears. At Welcome Weekend, I still give parents my home phone number, much to the horror of many colleague presidents.

Like most student affairs professionals, I am process driven. I understand my role as one of managing boundaries within which the primary tasks of the university, teaching and learning, can proceed without distraction. Perhaps that is why so many student affairs types, like me, move from position to position so readily, because we are intrigued by the integration of programs and services. It also explains why, as president, I prioritize strategic planning above all else, except students.

Students come first on my agenda, in my budget, and as my primary measure of success. Had I not started out in student affairs, I doubt that I would have had the skills or comfort level to work with the complexity of student needs and issues that a president faces today. I know individual students by name, so I often use their stories to make a point or activate the conscience of a donor. And, when the going gets tough, as it does in a multi-constituency setting like a university, I remind myself and the group with whom I am wrestling that *it is not about us.*

> "Student affairs work tests you and weeds out the wimps."

Of course, having the resilience to lead is as critical as skills and perspective. Student affairs work tests you and weeds out the wimps. I was 22 years old the first (and only) time that I had to tell a father that his daughter committed suicide. In 22 years as a president, few challenges have matched that moment. And, as a consequence, I lead differently. I have greater patience for helicopter parents; I believe in second chances; and I try to keep my door and my heart open.

I approach the presidency as a lifestyle, not a job. That, too, is an artifact of student affairs, with its long hours and playful elements. It was during those early years of managing crowds and mediating conflicts that I developed the mantra that has sustained me in difficult moments: *Absorb chaos, respond calmly, and over time, you will build confidence in the organization and your leadership.* I also learned not to take myself too seriously, which was essential when trying to corral inebriated students while standing knee deep in waste, after they had flushed all the toilets in the residence hall at once.

Given all the above, you can imagine my distress as a young student activities director, when I first discovered that my Myers-Briggs type was INTJ: an introverted, intuitive, thinker, judger. Where was the touchy-feely extrovert that I associated with the profession? Student affairs trained that part of me, but it was the other, the self-reliant pragmatist, that equipped me for the hard and lonely decisions that define a president, that and the promise of a Catholic, Dominican education.

THE MISSION FACTOR

As the saying goes, *I came for the responsibility; I stayed for the mission,* one that not only aligns with, but also empowers the practice of intentional student development and advocacy. So many of the issues that challenge university presidents today — access, affordability, inclusion, Title IX — are student-related and can be addressed within the context of Catholic Social Teaching. Without a background in student affairs, I might not have fully understood the importance of the co-curriculum in advancing social justice and civic engagement. It is also less likely that my cabinet would include a vice president for mission or a chief diversity officer, voices that I value.

Of course, there is a reason that more student affairs professionals end up as Catholic university presidents. At heart, Catholic education is about character formation and that is our business. The challenge, then, is to ensure that goal is foundational across the university and that it ties back to the history and religious tradition of the university. At Dominican, we offer a first-year faculty seminar, *What Matters,* and a yearly residential retreat, *Contemplating Life's Calling,* to encourage faculty ownership of mission. Student affairs staff often teach the teachers, in practice, if not formally.

Many of the innovations in undergraduate pedagogy today that build character and conscience have their roots in student affairs: internships, community-based learning, service immersion trips, intrusive advising, etc. As a president with a firsthand sensitivity to the university pecking order, I try to give credit where credit is due and to identify student affairs professionals as partners with faculty in the process of shaping hearts and minds.

My student affairs years were not spent at a Catholic university, so I cannot speak from the trenches. But I do know from more recent experience that faith and leadership are inseparable in the delivery of Catholic higher education. You model what you believe. Had it not been for the integrating vision of feminism and justice that I found among the Dominicans, I would not have the adult Catholic faith that I have today. I would not be the president that I am, able to grapple with complex contemporary issues in a Catholic context and, when necessary, in good conscience, to push the envelope for the sake of relevance.

Somewhere between my early years in student affairs and my first decade as a president, I ultimately came to understand my work as a vocation. The joy that I still feel working with students became an anchor for the never-ending challenges of the presidency, and the two just made more sense in the context of a Catholic Dominican university. It all became that much more meaningful and potent. Right now, I have mobilized that sense of purpose and my still ferocious appetite for responsibility to advocate for the rights of undocumented students — and so, the work comes full circle.

IN CONCLUSION

Having said all of that, here is a bit of advice for student affairs professionals working in Catholic higher education today. First, if you do not believe fully in the mission of the institution, even when you are being its loving critic, then *get out of Dodge*. It is not enough to be a good practitioner. You must care.

I would advise you to take full advantage of the important teaching role that student affairs can play in the character formation of students. Do not talk vaguely about the co-curriculum. Identify clear learning goals, activities, and metrics. Help your president articulate the distinctive advantages of a Catholic education, and make yourself indispensable in its delivery.

Also, see your field through your president's eyes. Of course, we are interested in student development, but we also are concerned about retention and, ultimately, about strong student outcomes.

If you can help it, never surprise the boss. Student affairs can be messy and unpredictable. A president manages better and can be more supportive if he or she has room to maneuver. Arrive with solutions that advance the mission of the university, not just problems. And finally, most presidents who started in student affairs will always be deans of students at heart, so include us in the fun stuff, too, if only because it helps us tell your story.

Donna M. Carroll is president of Dominican University in River Forest, Illinois.

CHAPTER 2

Student Affairs:
The Beating Heart of the Academy

Bassam M. Deeb

I discovered my love for student affairs while attending a large state university for my undergraduate degree in geography. Like many students, I felt a need to belong, to find my place in a vast and complex institution of higher education. I signed up for a peer advising class and began working in academic advising and student orientation. Though a student myself, I found fulfillment in guiding my peers through their academic careers. I had been deeply impacted years earlier by a similar mentoring relationship.

As a young man, newly immigrated to the United States from war-torn Lebanon, an advisor at the adult learning center in my new hometown steered me toward my high school diploma. Her advice and guidance would ensure my long-term success. I realized during college that I, too, could pursue a career helping others reach their potential. This inspired me to pursue a master's degree in student personnel.

Like so many of us with a passion for higher education, I met people along the way who supported my development. My advisor during my master's program explained that, in student affairs, we are in the business of helping people. He was no exception. He pointed out my gifts and abilities and, once my core courses were complete, strongly encouraged internships. Through his prompting, I garnered three internships at different schools in student affairs and enrollment services. This diversity of experience made me much more marketable upon graduation.

With my degree in hand, I began applying for professional positions and landed a job as the director of advising and retention at Briar Cliff College (now a university) in Sioux City, Iowa. More than 1,000 miles from my home in Buffalo, New York, Briar Cliff is a Catholic institution in the Franciscan tradition. There I learned three important lessons that shaped my view and approach to student affairs.

First, while graduate school exposed me to student development theory and the holistic development of the student within an academic environment, at Briar Cliff I experienced firsthand how student affairs contributes to the Catholic mission.

> "These experiences shaped my understanding of the student affairs function and through them I formed a profound commitment to serving students."

The Sisters of St. Francis modeled the spirit of the profession at the academy and, more specifically, in the Division of Student Affairs. They aligned their work with the core values of the college — service, caring, and openness. The sisters' formation, as religious members, taught them many of the same principles I learned in graduate school. While I had knowledge, they showed me how to live out the values of the mission in a practical way. Whether they were serving as leaders, fiercely advocating for programs to develop students holistically, or sitting with a student one-on-one to help them through difficulty, they modeled the kind of professional I wanted to be. As a result, I set out to merge my training with the positive behaviors I witnessed in the sisters.

The second experience at Briar Cliff that shaped my view of student affairs was interacting with Catholic campus ministry, a functionality fully integrated in the Division of Student Affairs. In their efforts to help others, they worked side by side with individuals of other faith traditions and those who professed no religious affiliation at all. This diverse group of individuals worked together to serve our local community through both individual and group projects and our fully integrated campus-wide food drive. The campus ministry staff focused on the spiritual development of all students, while embodying a passion for Catholic Social Teaching rooted in the Franciscan tradition, with an emphasis on caring for all God's people regardless of belief. I was inspired.

Lastly, my first professional position in higher education taught me the importance of creating opportunities for others to serve the community through the Catholic university. At Briar Cliff, we opened pathways for individuals into the academy. Furthermore, the university community collectively committed to St. Francis' vision to serve the basic needs of those in our midst through service projects in nearby neighborhoods.

Those early years at Briar Cliff set the stage for doctoral studies in higher education: 24 years and counting in higher education, 11 years as a senior student affairs officer, and now a college president. These experiences shaped my understanding of the student affairs function and through them I formed a profound commitment to serving students. My experiences were influenced by the 1937 *Student Personnel Point of View* and the companion document, the 1997 *Principles of Good Practice in Student Affairs*. The latter, released at a joint meeting of NASPA and ACPA, of which I was a part, continues to guide my approach to higher education administration, whether in the role of senior student affairs officer or college president. Combined experiences in the public and private sectors of higher education challenged me to take the best of both worlds and envision a student affairs model that is transformative for students, a model that achieves the following:

1. *Educating the whole person:* As higher education administrators, we must consider the intellectual, physical, social, and spiritual needs of our students, with a special emphasis on the latter. In my experience, students' spiritual needs are often the most neglected aspect of education in the broader industry.

2. *Inspiring citizenship:* We must capitalize on the opportunity to inspire students to become citizens that fully participate in community, from caring for those who are less fortunate to engaging in social and political reform to improve society and the lives of individuals.

3. *Instilling a desire for continuous improvement:* As students engage in a robust learning process, we reveal the transformative value of education. We must instill in them a yearning for lifelong learning — to learn about themselves; develop their craft or profession; remain open to others' ideas, beliefs, cultures, and methods; and seek to adapt to the ever-changing world in which we live.

4. *Developing a strong moral compass:* My life has been dramatically impacted by the Maronite Rite, an eastern Catholic faith developed in the fourth century in what is today Lebanon and Syria. This congregational movement relied on the monastic life and a strongly held Catholic belief to constantly interact with and adjust to other faiths and Christian traditions in the Middle East. I learned to remain rooted in my values and morals, not be afraid, and stand firm in my beliefs while honoring those different from mine. Catholic higher education is uniquely poised to lead such a movement.

Though not one of my original goals, after developing a wealth of experience in student affairs and teasing out my philosophies of the profession, a college presidency became a possibility. When I entered higher education administration in the mid-1980s, the number of college presidents whose experience came from student affairs could be counted on one hand. Higher education in general, while it pursues the transformation of students, is slow to change itself. The road to the college presidency then, and still today, is often reached through academic leadership.

Throughout my non-traditional career path to the presidency, I worked hard to develop and live out the values outlined herein. I often considered the wisdom one of my mentors shared when he encouraged me to be ready to serve my institution in any way possible. This helped me shift positions and pursue opportunities that offered insight into the structure of higher education. Over the years, I worked in, or supervised, nearly every operation in student affairs, including enrollment services. I established a non-profit organization with the sole purpose of developing, building, and operating student housing. I served as interim chief academic officer for two semesters, giving me greater insight into academic affairs. This combination of experiences led me to believe that a presidency was possible.

The opportunity to become a college president at a small Catholic college has been the ideal professional twist to an eclectic administrative career. Twenty-six years after taking my first job at a small Catholic college in Iowa, which had transitioned from a women's junior college to a coeducational, career-focused university rooted in the liberal arts, I joined Trocaire College in Buffalo, New York. I found myself back at a Catholic institution that started as a school to educate women religious for service in ministries but now enrolls lay men and women in career-focused programs with a foundation in the liberal arts. Rooted in the mission of the Sisters of Mercy, Trocaire College brings back fond memories of the Franciscan tradition in which I began my career: traditions that lead us to focus on transforming students' lives, caring for and nurturing those who most need us, and preparing students for service in the universal community.

One of my early mentors said, "A successful student affairs operation is the beating heart of the academy." Student affairs is just that. The values and practices that a great student affairs division integrates throughout the campus community are akin to the life-blood, oxygen, and nutrients that the heart pumps throughout the human body. An affirmed, renewed, and transformed student is the ultimate goal of the Catholic college or university. Without an inspirational, comprehensive, and successful student affairs operation, the entire academy suffers.

After four years as a college president, my love for student affairs remains. I believe the student affairs profession sits at the heart of the institution. It is often the best place to develop the future leaders of our industry. Higher education requires us to be efficient managers, able to steward complex financial operations while remaining quantifiably accountable. We must juggle the demands of multiple internal and external constituencies while remaining aware and responsive to the ever-expanding influence of government entities.

Yet we must, at all times, dedicate significant time and energy toward those who need our support most — our students. The college president who is deeply rooted in the student affairs profession brings with him or her a unique ability to lead and manage the institution while setting a firm focus on serving students. It has been my joy and pleasure to fulfill that role.

Bassam M. Deeb is president of Trocaire College in Buffalo, New York.

CHAPTER 3

Providing for Formation and Enabling the 'Authentic Self': The Work of Student Affairs

John J. DeGioia

Student affairs plays an invaluable and irreplaceable role in supporting the most important task of colleges and universities: the formation of our students — the integration of their intellect, character, and spirit. This work of supporting formation is carried out via an array of offices, programs, policies, and practices, some of which can be in tension with each other. The arena of student affairs intends to respond to the complexity of new, often conflicting, demands placed on academic communities — and hence, the elements that constitute it can themselves appear complex, even conflicting.

For more than four decades, Georgetown University has been my home, and from 1985 to 1992, I was privileged to serve as the university's dean of students. In that role, and in my role as Georgetown president, I have come to know the extraordinary contributions that student affairs makes to the life of a university community.

Consider the kinds of obligations that student affairs routinely deal with on a college or university campus. Student affairs, as currently constituted, has four responsibilities:

The first is in providing "order" for day-to-day student life. The foundation for this order is the policies for encouraging responsible behavior in the conduct of everyday life. Student affairs not only sets guidelines for that behavior but also ensures that it is carried out. That means being attentive to those who are not living within the guidelines of acceptable behavior, identifying those who may pose a threat to themselves and others, and ensuring that students "do no harm."

Second, closely connected to the insistence on enabling students to fully embrace and participate in its "order," is the crucial nature of providing a safety net that addresses the range of challenges that are found in every student community.

> "Student affairs is not only about what *not* to do; it is about what is possible *to* do. "

Consider the following characteristics of a typical community of young people:

•   A third of students between the ages of 18 and 24 will cope with the clinical signs of depression (Henriques, 2014);

•   Fifteen percent of our women are managing an eating disorder (National Institutes of Health, 2012);

•   Between 20 and 30 percent of college women have confronted unwanted acts of sexual assault (New, 2015);

•   More than 10 percent of our students engage in heavy drinking (NSDUH, 2014).

Student affairs, given these realities, typically manages a network of individuals and resources that seeks to recognize the signs of a student coping with risky behavior and provide the appropriate intervention that will help him or her address them. Student affairs, then, not only identifies problems; it seeks to ameliorate them.

Third, student affairs is not simply a monitoring agency. Student affairs provides multiple and diverse opportunities for the development of leadership skills through a broad range of student clubs and organizations. With programs ranging from community service to artistic performance, from cultural clubs and a diversity of media organizations — newspapers, radio, television, film, and gaming — student affairs creates the framework that helps students balance their academic pursuits with meaningful extra- and co-curricular activities. Student affairs is not only about what *not* to do; it is about what is possible *to* do. It is this combination of insisting on having students conform to the norms of the university and, at the same time, offering enrichment of their experiences *as* students beyond those captured in their classroom learning, that makes student affairs an important, if complex, arena within the institution.

Finally, when structured well, student affairs contributes to *building a community* within the school. When colleges and universities are at their best, they provide an inclusive context for students to learn more about themselves and to engage with those around them — students, faculty, and staff, across differences of identity.

STUDENT AFFAIRS AND FORMATION, IN CONTEXT

To understand more deeply the role of student affairs, it is important to understand the context in which its work takes place. Three elements shape the university, its purpose, and its values, and these have defined our identities for the past millennia: (1) We support the formation of young people; (2) we support the inquiry of our faculty; and (3) we, as institutions, contribute to the common good. These three elements are mutually reinforcing, inextricably linked, and cannot be unbundled without risking irreparable damage to the integrity of the enterprise.

The element of the academy that is given the most attention and support by student affairs is the *work* of formation. Formation can occur in many different settings: in religious orders, in military training, in entrepreneurial ventures. What distinguishes the university is its emphasis on knowledge. Particularly salient is the accumulation of that knowledge and how that understanding of the accumulation of knowledge contributes to our understanding of the world in which we live. We believe the acquisition and dissemination, the discovery and construction, the interpretation and conservation of knowledge together determine the orientation of the university — it is what we do; it is what we contribute to the students who weave in and out and to the larger environments in which we are situated. We introduce students to disciplines and methodologies for engaging in the work of knowing. This commitment to knowledge differentiates the university from other settings where formation is also present; it makes the free enquiry of knowledge an essential feature of the work of formation.

Moreover, universities provide a place for protecting and nurturing resources of incomparable value for deepening self-understanding, self-awareness, and self-knowledge — resources that support the interior work of making meaning of one's life. We seek to provide a context for our students to become their most *authentic* selves. Such a goal can only be attained through demanding interior work. An "authentic self" is one living in accord with one's most deeply held values. Our decisions and actions are informed by these values, these goods. We seek alignment between these goods and our decisions and actions.

All of us struggle to align our decisions and actions with the deepest goods that animate our lives. It is a critical mission of the university to enable an authentic self to emerge and to enable that authentic self, through what we introduce within the university, to flourish. Students begin this work of formation through exposure to what they learn and experience in their studies. Formation helps encourage an interior freedom that, when coupled with free enquiry, helps break through blocks to authenticity.

23

How do we understand the nature of the interior lives of our young people? How are they making sense of our world? What effect do new technologies of connecting with one another, of social networking, have on their ways of making meaning in their lives? How are their imaginations being formed, and how do they understand the depth and breadth of their possibilities? Student affairs plays a critical role in helping answer these questions.

We may not yet know what goods — what values and beliefs — are most dear to us. We may be engaged in the discovery and discernment of these goods. We may have a clear commitment and yet lack the virtues that can sustain us in the day-to-day struggle to decide and act in accord with these goods. We may need a community to enable us to find the interior resources to live authentically.

At a Catholic university, we believe in the presence of the Spirit, animating the works and days of our communities. We have a sacramental imagination, seeking the sacred in our experiences. We explore the boundaries between reason and revelation, between "Athens and Jerusalem," without diminishing the authority of either. A Jesuit university places special emphasis on, in the Latin, *cura personalis*, that is, the care for each person within the community.

A liberal education, a way of life, is the great gift we can provide our students based on the openness that scholastic free enquiry enables. We introduce them to the university way of life, one that aims to integrate intellect, character, and spirit in its formation endeavor, supported by the work of student affairs, with its multiple intersections with students themselves.

For what ties together the formation, with critical support from student affairs, and the emphasis on interior freedom, and the essential connection to free enquiry of scholars, is the *purpose* of the endeavor. It is more than the individual's work — one's pursuit of interior freedom, the free enquiry of scholastic interests. This is all *for* something. There is a larger purpose implicit in this path: a commitment to contributing to the common good.

John J. DeGioia is president of Georgetown University in Washington, DC.

REFERENCES

Henriques, G. "The College Mental Health Crisis." *Psychology Today.* Retrieved from https://www.psychology today.com/blog/theory-knowledge/201402/the-college-student-mental-health-crisis.

Multi-Service Eating Disorders Association (MEDA).

New, J. "One in Four?" *Inside Higher Ed.* September 22, 2015. Retrieved from https://www.insidehighered.com/news/2015/09/22/nearly-1-4-college-women-say-they-have-been-sexually-assaulted-survey-finds.

2014 National Survey on Drug Use and Health (NSDUH). *Substance Abuse and Mental Health Services Administration (SAMHSA).* Retrieved from http://www.samhsa.gov/data/sites/default/files/NSDUH-DetTabs2014/NS-DUH-DetTabs2014.htm#tab6-90b.

CHAPTER 4

Pope Francis: A Model of Leadership and Management at Catholic Institutions and a Guide for Senior Student Affairs Officers

James J. Maher, CM

A faculty colleague from Niagara University's College of Business Administration recently shared with me a piece from the *Harvard Business Review* in which Pope Francis was referred to, in a positive manner, as a manager and leader. In my 10 years of reading the periodical, I cannot recall a pope ever being referenced in such a way.

People often point to Pope Francis's adept understanding of symbols and, more so, his use of these symbols to effectively advance values, dialogue, and mutual understanding. Frequently lost, however, is Pope Francis's managerial ability, the day-to-day work and ministry in which he seeks to move the Catholic Church forward by embracing its traditions and seeking appropriate relevance and fidelity to teaching and impact.

In his book, *The Holy Longing: The Search for a Christian Spirituality*, Fr. Ronald Rolheiser, OM, notes that authentic spirituality must address the "bread and butter" issues of human life. From my perspective, I surmise that Pope Francis is seeking to link the Catholic Church's faith and fidelity in Christ to the most vexing human matters of our time, those that may be considered the "bread and butter" issues of the 21st century.

University leaders and managers can benefit from Pope Francis's example by developing a sense of living spirituality among the student affairs sector. I suggest that this can be accomplished by reflecting on three concepts: a spirituality of accompaniment, a spirituality of administration, and a spirituality of the academy and workplace.

Several years ago, I was asked by the Vincentian provincial to participate in a project that facilitated the sharing of some of the Eastern Province of the Congregation of the Mission's endowment with the six poorest provinces within the worldwide Vincentian community. I was assigned to work with the Province of Indonesia to help it determine how the gifts would be utilized. Our first objective was to establish endowed funds. The second task was to purposely direct those funds in ways that aligned with our Vincentian charism, such as funding works for people living in poverty and supporting education of the clergy and lay ecclesial leaders.

I spent two weeks on the island of Java, Indonesia, visiting Vincentian houses and ministries. As I was departing the country, the provincial at the time, Fr. Sad Budianto, CM, walked with me to my gate at the airport and then proceeded to wait with me until my plane arrived. Numerous times I suggested that it would be appropriate for him to carry on with his day, because I was an experienced traveler and knew he was very busy.

Gently, Fr. Budianto would say, "I will accompany you." Those four words remain with me today, and when I find myself too focused on completing comparatively menial tasks, I am reminded to accompany the people I am seeking to serve. Similarly, Pope Francis has challenged priests, bishops, deacons, sisters, brothers, and lay church leaders to be present for those who need us most. Extending this into Catholic colleges and universities, students should not only feel the effects of our policies, programs, and services, but also feel the power of our presence.

Senior student affairs officers must make it their aim to cultivate a working spirituality of accompanying students throughout their four-year journeys, which are replete with many wonderful blessings and personal development challenges.

College campuses, by their very layout, make it possible to conduct most student affairs meetings behind closed doors. Yet, while this may occasionally be necessary, I believe that Pope Francis has raised the bar for leaders at Catholic institutions to be accessible to people, accompanying them with a dynamic and regular presence.

As a former senior student affairs officer, I worked hard to be present on campus by attending various programs and events. In addition, I strived to be present in the daily lives of students without intruding, the opportunities for which may arise from eating in the dining hall, having coffee in public areas and, when appropriate, meeting with staff in spaces that allowed for student interaction. My experiences taught me that the policies, programs, and services of the division were positively impacted because of my regular contact with students, faculty, administrators, and staff.

It is critical for senior student affairs officers to construct a culture of accompanying students. Many individuals who work in the sector do this quite well; they are excited by the prospect of engaging students. By setting a proper example of accompanying others, leaders will make it part of the fabric of the culture of their student affairs sectors to accompany students on their journeys through this pivotal juncture in their lives.

When we develop a culture of accompaniment, we help students grow in freedom and responsibility, walking with them as they seek to progress in their search for truth, beauty, love, justice, and mercy. Such an approach calls us back to the core of our work, to help students embrace and seek to develop themselves academically, personally, socially, and spiritually. Senior student affairs officers need to view their offices as the doors to initiating engagement and accompaniment.

A spirituality of administration is another tenet that must be reflected by senior student affairs professionals at Catholic colleges and universities. At the core of this concept resides the belief that administration is a labor of servant leadership that allows the Catholic and student development missions to flourish.

In some respects, there is a mundane character to this work, requiring discipline and regular patterns of committed work. In many instances, this is work that goes largely unseen and occupies a formidable time commitment. Some commentators note that while Pope Francis so clearly understands and embraces the power of personal and public symbols, he is also a deeply dedicated administrator. It is observed that he spends much of his morning and other parts of his day reviewing reports and fulfilling the often-thankless tasks of reading, studying, and preparing for meetings. Such an approach recognizes that a spirituality of administration seeks not to make administration its end; rather, in the words of St. Paul in the letter of Timothy, to allow truth, beauty, and God's spirit to flourish.

I have discovered elements of spirituality of administration during my time as a senior student affairs officer and, now, as a university president. The following are some concrete ways that I have found this spirituality of administration to be life giving:

First, surround yourself with immensely gifted people, professionals who have expertise and specialized knowledge that you do not possess. In my years serving as vice president of student affairs, I surrounded myself with people who had great proficiency in student wellness and counseling, residence life, career services, student programing, pluricultural issues, and other specialized areas. I often learned much from them, and such an approach allowed them to utilize their expertise. Rest assured, your authority as a vice president will be strengthened, not weakened.

Second, challenge yourself and those you supervise to a culture of excellence and servant leadership. Lead by example in your commitment to excellence and allow others to see, in your administration, that no task is beneath you.

Third, recruit and hire student affairs professionals who seek the opportunity to fulfill their personal goals in congruence with our Catholic mission. Throughout my

> "Challenge yourself to a spirituality of administration that empowers others in the mission of student affairs."

career, I have been edified by the commitment to mission evidenced by my colleagues, finding at times my own commitment to mission paling in comparison. The greatest gift you can provide others seeking careers in student affairs is to present a spirituality of administration that unlocks the beauty of the gift of administration to advance our mission of student affairs and Catholicity.

Do not be threatened by the gifts and expertise of those you supervise. I have witnessed instances in which a sector was held back simply because the lead administrator was threatened by the expertise, creativity, and giftedness of direct reports. Harnessing the collective gifts of the people around you will allow your sector to function at far greater heights. Challenge yourself to a spirituality of administration that empowers others in the mission of student affairs to attain outcomes facilitated by you, but for which you receive no credit. That which embodies transcendent and eternal values is the highest level of spirituality of administration.

Finally, in his early work on *The Seven Habits of Highly Successful People*, the late Stephen Covey encouraged his audience to visualize their funeral. The most pressing question Covey raised centered on what would be said about you at the end of your life. It is likely that such a practice is directly related to the philosophy of beginning with the end in mind. Translating that to student affairs, ask yourself as a senior officer: When I leave this position, what will people say about me?

Undoubtedly, all of us would like to have outstanding outcomes in key student satisfaction areas. Yet, I would posit that the most important work is not simply achieving results but, also, forming a community of the workplace. As a former senior student affairs officer and current university president, the core of what I do across campus resides in creating an environment and workplace in which people can actualize their personal mission within the context of our Catholic mission. Our work as leaders at Catholic institutions is not simply to create dynamic teams; it is also to create a community of bondedness by sharing our work, relationships, and mission and seeking to provide eternal purpose and meaning in life.

The creation of a community of the workplace and academy requires these essential elements:

- *First, a high-trust environment in which open, respectful, and honest dialogue occurs without the threat of reprisal.* As leaders, community begins to take foot when we commit to developing an environment that is not only safe but also where critical feedback and dialogue are welcomed. It begins with leadership modeling trust.

- *Second, a community in which listening abounds.* A disciplined and developed leader does not need to win the argument. He or she can be quiet and listen, ask pointed and direct questions rather than refute assumptions. By engaging in this practice, I have found myself led into deeper truth.

- *Third, open and honest communication is critical to fruitful relationships with members of the university community.* I have observed that the most effective leaders deliver difficult news in the context of being in relationship with others. Student affairs professionals do this with regularity and, thus, need to be models for administrators, staff, and faculty.

- We all experience times when we lose sight of our purpose and wonder why we chose a vocation in student affairs. Work in student affairs is life in the trenches: the gritty, everyday spirituality to which Pope Francis calls us. It is accompanying our students through the ups and downs, through the unexpected and the mundane. It is here that we become the "bread and butter" presence that makes a lasting difference in their lives.

Rev. James J. Maher, CM, is president of Niagara University in Niagara Falls, New York.

REFERENCES

Covey, S. (2004). *The 7 Habits of Highly Effective People: Powerful Lessons in Personal Change.* New York: Free Press.

Hamel, G. (14 April 2015). "The 15 Diseases of Leadership, According to Pope Francis." *Harvard Business Review.* Retrieved from https://hbr.org/2015/04/the-15-diseases-of-leadership-according-to-pope-francis.

Rolheiser, R. (2014). *The Holy Longing: The Search for a Christian Spirituality.* New York: Image.

CHAPTER 5

Job or Vocation: The Transformation of a Student Affairs Professional

Robert A. Pastoor

"The president is in charge of the Catholic mission of the institution." As I sit in the president's chair of a Catholic college, I am reminded daily of this quote from an ACCU meeting. Through my student affairs work, I have come to see our mission as one to fully develop the mind, body, and soul of every student in our care. Relationship building, whether inside or outside the classroom, is the core of the educational process. We have a duty, derived from our Catholic mission, to serve one another with dignity and respect, to serve the Church, to serve the disenfranchised and marginalized within our society, and to serve the world as a whole.

Five decades ago, when my career in Catholic higher education began, I knew little about the connection between student affairs, mission, and the Catholic Intellectual Tradition. Like others who ultimately found themselves in student affairs work, I entered college with a very different plan for my life. My path began as an undergraduate resident assistant, with no formal training, taking care of issues in the hall. I became a resident director while earning my M.Ed. in counseling. My first job in student affairs was as an assistant dean of students, which culminated with me as a vice president for student affairs for 24 years. Like many of my contemporaries, I learned on the job, reading journal articles, and through my membership in professional associations such as NASPA, ACPA, ASACCU, and JASPA. Today, learning on the job has been replaced with master's and doctoral programs available in fields that prepare students for varied and specific roles within student affairs.

Initially, I did not see my work in student affairs as a calling or a vocation. I viewed it as a job that I enjoyed, a career in which I could interact with students and help them process their lives in meaningful ways. It was the 1970s, a time filled with demonstrations, alcohol and drug abuse, and freedoms not previously seen on college campuses. These changes in student conduct precipitated the birth of student development theory.

Student affairs professionals began to view themselves as educators in the broader scheme of higher education. The University 101 programs developed by Dr. John Gardner helped students navigate the world of higher education. Educational programs were designed that delved into student development issues based on the preeminent work of Arthur Chickering, M. Lee Upcraft, George Kuh and Elizabeth Whitt, Marcia Baxter Magolda, and Lawrence Kohlberg. Student affairs professionals were invited to teach undergraduate students, such as resident assistants, peer mentors, peer leaders, and students enrolled in first-year seminar classes about these innovative theories, thus enabling students to explore and reflect on the purpose and greater meaning of their lives.

Sharing student affairs/development theories with my academic colleagues led to rich discussions. As a team, we developed engaging means of providing a holistic education for our students. It was the beginning of student affairs and academic affairs designing collaborative approaches and viewing one another as partners and educators.

I could be describing the life of a student affairs professional during that era at any public or private college or university in the country. I saw my role as one of carrying out my assigned duties and responsibilities. I gave little thought to the mission of the institution. My job was interchangeable with any student affairs position in the country. During my 16 years leading a division of student affairs at a Catholic college, two monumental events occurred that led me to change the way I viewed my work — allowing me to see it as a calling, a vocation.

The first was my introduction to *Ex corde Ecclesiae*. For many of us, the document had little to do with our work, because the scope of discussions centered on the *mandatum* contained therein. Unfortunately, during the lengthy and ongoing discussions about the breadth and beauty of *Ex corde Ecclesiae*, the relevance with which the document spoke to all areas within the purview of student affairs was lost. Dialogues about the meaning of being a Catholic institution, in light of *Ex corde Ecclesiae*, were carried on throughout the United States by Catholic colleges and universities. Sadly, those discussions were limited to the academic side of the house. It was reading the document on my own that allowed me to see student affairs work in a larger context. I began to appreciate the magnitude of change it brought to student affairs and the significant impact it could have on my own work.

My second and more profound change occurred when I further developed and gained clarity through my participation in the Institute for Student Affairs at Catholic Colleges (ISACC), a weeklong immersion into the Catholic Intellectual Tradition and student affairs work. Full discussions took place around *Gaudium et Spes: The Pastoral Constitution of the Church in the Modern World*. The week included talks about Church history and Church teaching on human sexuality. These were discussions that had not occurred in my theology classes in college nor among my peers at Catholic colleges and universities. A new world opened for me that brought into focus the mission of the Catholic college and my work in student affairs. I learned how deeply they were intertwined. That initial week as a participant, and the subsequent three years of working with ISACC, allowed me to see the Catholic foundation of student affairs and its meaning at a Catholic college. It was no longer about simply telling students what they could or could not do, whether it involved sexual issues, or alcohol, or other ethical issues. This information and understanding provided me a context for broader discussions about policies that existed on campus and how they related to the mission of the college.

My life as a vice president for student affairs, and as a person, fundamentally changed after reading *Ex corde Ecclesiae* and participating in ISACC. One of the beauties of student affairs work is the opportunity it provides to build relationships with students and faculty. These relationships are often long-lasting and bring meaning to my work. The work I did with ISACC enabled me to build relationships on a more intimate level. I was able to speak from a knowledge base that I had not previously possessed. I was compelled to share about areas such as faith and reason. As a result, my faith life grew and intensified, and I was invited to speak with students about the development of their faith lives. This became part of my personal and professional journey, one that I have shared openly. As I contemplated my role within my family, my school, and society at large, I no longer viewed my job simply as work but rather as a vocation.

> "One of the beauties of student affairs work is the opportunity it provides to build relationships with students and faculty."

As a college president, I can share my knowledge of student development and student affairs through the lens of Catholic identity as it relates to mission, thereby building a vision for the college as a Catholic college. Many issues that face colleges today exist outside the realm of academics. They exist in our residence halls, on our fields and courts, and in the intimacy of friendships. These issues touch upon human interaction, demanding respect for every human being regardless of race, creed, religion, ethnic origin, socio-economic background, gender, or sexual orientation. They touch on the development of one's conscience and ethical behavior and upon the meaning of one's life, as an individual, and as a member of a community of learners. These challenges are not new to colleges and universities. The marriage of the Catholic Intellectual Tradition

35

and the development of student affairs offers illumination and a means of addressing the complex issues that unite rather than divide. As president of my institution, the responsibility for the college's mission is mine, and living that mission has been the cornerstone of my journey of faith.

Robert A. Pastoor is president of Saint Joseph's College in Rensselaer, Indiana.

CHAPTER 6

The Roles of Residence Hall Staff Members in the Mission of the Catholic University

Mark L. Poorman, CSC

At the beginning of each academic year, I have the privilege of addressing our hall directors, assistant hall directors, and resident assistants during their hall staff training. Having spent 27 years living in residence halls, first as a hall director and later, a chaplain in residence, as well as serving for 11 years as a vice president for student affairs, I consider myself familiar with the highs and lows of life in a residence hall. And as a president, I am firmly convinced that it is in those hallowed hallways that some of our students' greatest learning takes place. In the talk, I reinforce the ideas that residential life is a cornerstone of our Catholic mission to make Christ present to the students and that our fundamental purpose as a Catholic university is to create Christian communities in our halls, where we aspire to provide not only intellectual but also moral and spiritual formation. Some of that formation occurs during those infamous 3:00 a.m. conversations in the residence halls, conversations that not only will our students remember, but that also will play a key role in helping them discern their identity during this four-year bridge between adolescence and adulthood. Often those conversations are with friends and roommates. But some of the most formative middle-of-the-night conversations take place with members of our hall staffs. And, as I convey to our hall staffs, theirs is the incredibly unique and challenging position of serving simultaneously as minister, educator, and professional to our students.

As someone whose academic background is in ethics, and whose areas of study include professional ethics, I am keenly interested in the unusual and demanding work done by our hall staffs. Professional ethics is easiest to consider when people have clear roles and boundaries in their occupations. Working in the residence halls requires intentional blurring of those lines: There is an enormous overlap of roles with our hall staff living and working as students, employees, staff members, friends, peers, disciplinarians, counselors, and mentors, just to mention a few roles. That is both the genius and the challenge of our residence hall system. It can only work with individuals who not only accept the burden of balancing those many roles, but who, in fact, also view that juggling act as the very source of their success in forming residence hall communities where real growth can take place.

> "As Christians, we are living to be the face of Christ for others."

MINISTERS

Especially during training and early in the academic year, I get strange looks from hall staff members when I refer to them as "ministers." But that is, I believe, their first and foremost responsibility. The service they render is a direct extension of the Catholic mission of the university. If you examine the mission statement of almost any Catholic institution of higher education, you will likely find some version of three characteristics of Catholicism that have been formulated by Catholic theologian Richard McBrien: a sacramental vision, a principle of mediation, and community. These are key components of the foundation upon which our Catholic colleges and universities rest.

Catholicism prizes a *sacramental vision:* We believe that through the visible world in which we live, we come to know the invisible God. As Christians, we are living to be the face of Christ for others; in this case, the students we serve. Various people are the presence of God to others in differing ways. It never ceases to amaze me that the vastly disparate personalities within a given hall staff have a remarkable collective capacity to reach nearly all our students. The members of our hall staff bring to the position what and who they are, and Christ works through these unique personalities to reach the individual people who are entrusted to their care.

Catholics believe in the principle of *mediation;* which is like the sacramental vision with a small difference: The Catholic vision perceives God working *through* persons, events, and material things. In all those discrete events and happenings of a day, or a week, or a year, the hand of God is at work in the life of the individual student. As we all know, there are certain predictable and perennial things that happen on a university campus: first-year orientation, job searches, volunteer opportunities, commencement. The Catholic vision sees these and all the points in our lives as "moments of grace," where God is working in what are sometimes the strangest and most difficult circumstances. Why is this principle of mediation important to residential life? As ministers, our hall staffs are doing more than just counseling, policing, or hanging out. They live day-to-day with their senses tuned to the truth that God may be doing a new thing, a good thing, a *holy* thing in the lives of the students they serve and recognize that they may well be the agents for God's grace.

The Catholic vision of life embraces the notion of *community:* God's ways come to us through the communities in which we live. James Joyce once observed that when somebody says "Catholic," they mean "Here comes everybody." This kind of

38

community does not just tolerate others because they possess certain civil rights. Rather, it offers a total embrace of others simply because they are children of God. The reason residential life is such an integral part of our Catholic institutions is that community is one of the bedrocks of our Christian identity. A residential community is especially well-suited for providing its members an experience of the riches of the common life. Christianity is communal at its very core, and our residence halls are the natural extension of the community that Jesus created with the disciples and that has characterized the manifold forms of "church" ever since.

EDUCATORS

Too often there is a perception that education happens in the classroom, and fun happens in the residence hall. One would be forgiven for thinking so, because the education that happens in the residence hall is often tucked in among video game tournaments and free pizza. And yet, our residence halls exist, within the broader mission of our universities, to be places of teaching and learning that prepare our students to serve and lead; where personal faith and formation are taken seriously and infused throughout the entire institution. What we do in the halls is a direct extension of the core academic mission of the university. If you've spent any time teaching, you know that there are many ways that people learn. In the residence halls, our hall staff have opportunities that even the most accomplished and accessible faculty members don't have, and they are opportunities of which we must take advantage.

In my experience, the most effective resident assistants, assistant hall directors, and hall directors exhibit pedagogical qualities that help them do that. They believe that ideas have consequences. They are patient in their efforts to enlighten and guide other people. They are able to take the long view of how to get someone conceptually or developmentally from point A to point B. They are creative in their approaches to individuals' unique needs, but they also know how to mind the common good. They don't get overly discouraged by efforts to teach that are not well received. These are what truly make them educators.

PROFESSIONALS

Living and working in the residence halls is an around-the-clock job that demands our hall staff members offer their whole selves in service to our students. It is challenging and exhausting. And it offers that deep sense of joy and accomplishment that only the most difficult assignments can. As professionals in student services, our hall staff members are prized and treasured not just for what they do, but also for who they are. Their judgment is trusted, their competence is trusted, their care for others is trusted, and their reputation is trusted. Students, parents, and the university make acts of faith that members of our hall staffs are worth trusting. The fundamental responsibility of any professional is to live up to the faith that others have placed in them, to be competent and trustworthy. In both job performance and personal virtue, one must have integrity and be what he or she purports to be. As has been noted by others, the professional leader doesn't just *deliver* the message; he or she *is* the message. For many of our hall staff members, this position is their first entrance into the professional arena. For some students, it may be the first job they've had in which a good portion of the job description is simply being themselves.

With regard to competence, the professional has to have the skill and training to actually deliver the service that he or she promises to deliver. With regard to trustworthiness, the professional must be a person with certain virtues in order to fulfill their end of a covenant — honesty, fidelity, good judgment, perseverance, courage, hope, humility, to mention just a few. Our hall staff members must be people of competence and character so *that others* can place their trust in them.

CONCLUSION

My student affairs background has been invaluable to me as a university president. While our academic mission sits at the center of what we do, our residential mission plays a crucial role in fostering the community to support that academic mission. And it is our hall staff members — those ministers, educators, and professionals — who are responsible for bringing that mission to life for our students.

Rev. Mark L. Poorman, CSC, is president of the University of Portland in Portland, Oregon.

CHAPTER 7

Fostering Transformation through Both the Unexpected and the Mundane

Mark C. Reed

Imagine being the first lay president of a highly traditional Catholic, Jesuit university. You have been on the job for less than a month. Your office walls are still bare and the campus, in early August, is as quiet as can be. "Dr. Reed, the U.S. Secret Service is on the phone..."

With that, the focus on Saint Joseph's University as a Catholic, Jesuit institution was about to change forever. Pope Francis, on his September 2015 pilgrimage to the East Coast, was considering an interfaith visit to SJU. Saint Joseph's Institute for Jewish-Catholic Relations had been brought to the Pontiff's attention and it was now possible, perhaps even probable, that the Holy Father would come and bless a campus memorial of *Nostra Aetate*, the Vatican II document that transformed the relationship between the Catholic and Jewish faiths.

A single historic journey to the United States — with stops at the White House, a joint session of Congress, and the United Nations — might now include Saint Joseph's University. How does a president prepare for such a moment? How can it raise the Catholic, Jesuit profile of the institution? Most importantly, how is it made into a transformative experience for students, alumni, and the university overall?

"...And remember, Dr. Reed, there can be no public mention of a papal visit to your campus or, really, anyone for that matter. This is officially not a scheduled event, and should it become public, it will be cancelled."

In my earlier years as a student affairs professional, having spent the bulk of my career at Fairfield University, I had come to believe it was no longer possible to be surprised. As dean of students and later vice president for student affairs, I had heard it all. Individual student concerns, well-intended but hovering parents, ongoing sagas from residence life, and the ever-present community relations challenges make for an exceedingly full day.

In a way, every campus is its own small town (for some, not so small). The same triumphs and tragedies that exist in any population are present: in the

> "Our most significant opportunities can occur when students are vulnerable or even at risk."

confluence of young men and women taking the fast lane to adulthood; older professionals returning to school for one reason or another; administrators and staff in place to provide every kind of service; and, of course, faculty in their role at the heart of the enterprise.

It would be disingenuous of me to espouse a certain theory of student affairs practice, when my own management style was often trial and error. Few decisions in higher education, especially as they pertain to student organizations and conduct, are irreversible. One must be willing to adapt and sometimes even change direction at a moment's notice. I would add that a certain level of professional and even personal humility doesn't hurt.

As a mathematics major and later a calculus instructor at both Fairfield and Saint Joseph's, I often viewed student life as a math problem. We seek the greatest good for the greatest number of students. We understand there are few, if any, absolutes in our discipline. And we treat the inevitable exceptions to the many policies governing our actions as part of the "spirit" and not so much the "letter" of the law.

I believe the inherent non-conformity suggested by this last approach is one area in which Catholic — and in our case, Jesuit — institutions are distinct. We are, after all, mission driven, bringing with it all manner of contradictions between theory and day-to-day practicality.

The following language, for example, likely exists in some manner in all our mission statements: student-centered education; inclusive and diverse communities; care for the whole person; making ethical decisions; pursuing social justice. In a Jesuit setting, add the phrase "finding God in all things," and our marching orders are complicated indeed.

Admittedly, it isn't always easy "finding God" in those Monday morning incident reports. Yet I think most student affairs professionals would agree that our most significant opportunities can occur when students are vulnerable or even at risk. In the long run, it doesn't matter how they reach our doorstep. What matters more are the efforts at personal care and understanding — even if that care is disciplinary — that can shape an individual's growth for years to come. Or, as a parent once shared with me, "All kids need a pat on the back. Our job is figuring out when it should be the back or the backside." Maybe we should include that in the job description for all student affairs professionals.

Like any new president, I approached my first year at Saint Joseph's with energy and excitement. I was anxious to both learn and make a difference. I am especially proud to represent the student affairs profession in this role. And I was armed with all the data about my "customers" — the so-called Generation Z — suggesting traditional college and university presidents (or presidencies) might be a thing of the past.

In a recent study of today's 19-and-under set, the higher education marketing firm Ologie posits a simple bottom line from this next generation of undergraduates: "Talk to us based on our mindset," they say, "not our demographic. This means spending time to understand us and what it takes to get — and keep — our interest."

For me, this all crystalized on the last Sunday of September 2015. A pair of Saint Joseph's alumni and our best inside sources on the papal visit (one, the archdiocesan liaison to the Pontifical Council for the Family and the other, Philadelphia's co-chair of the 2015 World Meeting of Families) confirmed that a publicly unscheduled stop by Pope Francis was, in fact, still on the Holy Father's schedule. The mysterious Fiat, which passed right by our campus several times throughout the weekend, would be turning into the Chapel of St. Joseph parking lot on Sunday afternoon … as long as we didn't tell anyone…

So there I was welcoming the president and vice president of the SJU Student Senate to the President's Office earlier on Sunday afternoon. The two students were there under the pretense (really, a well-intentioned lie to preserve the confidentially of the "unscheduled" stop) of joining me in V.I.P. seats at the huge outdoor Papal Mass scheduled later that day in Philadelphia's Center City.

When told of the real purpose of their invitation, that they had been chosen to represent the student body and greet Pope Francis personally, at least one of the students broke down in a sweat and both were initially overwhelmed. Even more telling was the reaction that use of their cell phones would be prohibited. As Generation Z students remind us in numerous behavioral surveys, "We communicate constantly. [Our] digital connections with the world are essential. We want a personal experience."

By now, even a cell phone ban wasn't enough. The Holy Father's press secretary had mentioned Saint Joseph's University when speaking in Italian to reporters at nearby St. Charles Seminary. The faithful — in particular, our own students, alumni, and friends — converged on the *Nostra Aetate* memorial like a shrine. Who knew it was about to become one? (SJU's Institute for Jewish-Catholic Relations, founded in

1967 in response to the Second Vatican Council's historic declaration to re-establish and renew positive relations between Jews and Catholics, had commissioned the statue to commemorate the 50th anniversary of *Nostra Aetate*. It was installed and dedicated two days prior to the Pope's visit on campus. The keynote speaker at the dedication was Rabbi Abraham Skorka, an Argentinian Rabbi, friend, and colleague of Pope Francis. Coincidence, luck, or divine intervention?)

With the Secret Service nearly overcome by the growing crowds, a young Jesuit named Dan Joyce took to a bullhorn to help move onlookers back from the statue and clear a path for the Holy Father. Thousands of students, faculty, staff, and alumni pressed toward the spot while hundreds more hung from residence hall and office windows in the hope of glimpsing the Pontiff along what most presumed his campus path would be.

Yet there was still no official word from the Vatican. That is, until a SWAT team and mobile medical emergency crew arrived at a rear entrance to the site. The sudden presence of snipers on the roof of the student center seemed to quiet the crowd. Word came that the now-famous Fiat had exited St. Charles Seminary and was traveling the one-mile route toward SJU. Our moment had arrived. In full view of the world press and every major constituency of the university, history's first Jesuit pope was about to set foot on an American Jesuit campus for the very first time.

My own reaction was one of awe and inspiration. Part of me wondered, "If this happens in my first months as president, it can only go downhill from here…" Then reality set in. With "St. Joe's Loves the Pope" signs miraculously appearing in so many dorm room windows, Saint Joseph's University had made a new mark before an entire generation. Indeed, Saint Joseph's is where the Holy Father came to be among college students.

Two in particular, Student Senate president Nicholas Chingas '16 and vice president Natalie Roche '17, had greeted Pope Francis, looked into his eyes and he into theirs, and touched the moment of a lifetime. It wasn't digital, but it was as personal as could be. No one from Generation A through Z could be unmoved by the experience. It was also clear that my mission as president is to see the future through the eyes of our students. For a one-time student affairs professional who thought he couldn't be surprised any longer, it was the most meaningful reminder possible of the power of our work.

Mark C. Reed is president of Saint Joseph's University in Philadelphia, Pennsylvania.

SECTION TWO

Today's Landscape

CHAPTER 8   Setting the Stage: Results of a Survey of   **47**
Senior Student Affairs Officers

Sandra M. Estanek, Canisius College

CHAPTER 9   Getting Connected: Institutes, Organizations,   **53**
and Opportunities

*Alexandra Weber Bradley, Association of
Catholic Colleges and Universities*

CHAPTER 8

Setting the Stage: Results of a Survey of Senior Student Affairs Officers

Sandra M. Estanek

INTRODUCTION

To provide a context for the articles in this book, a new survey of senior student affairs officers at Catholic colleges and universities was conducted in March 2016. Similar surveys of SSAOs were published in 1990, 1996, and 2005. It was decided to construct the current survey along similar lines so that comparisons could be made. The survey collected demographic information on the responding institutions and the structure of student affairs. It profiled the senior student affairs officer and asked them three open-ended questions:

- How does the student affairs division contribute to the Catholic mission of the institution?

- What expectations do you have of staff related to the Catholic mission of the institution?

- What are some of the important issues related to Catholic mission?

Using a mailing list provided by the Association of Catholic Colleges and Universities, a survey was sent to 198 senior student affairs officers at Catholic colleges and universities. Responses were received from 103 participants, for a response rate of 52 percent. The survey allowed for respondents to skip questions so the number of responses for each question is not uniform.

FINDINGS

Institutional Profile

The majority (85 percent) of the institutions represented in the responses were small, with 5,000 or fewer undergraduate students. Fifteen percent (15 percent) had 5,000 or more undergraduate students. Forty-five percent (45 percent) of the respondents indicated that their undergraduate student body was between 40 percent and 60 percent Catholic. Twenty-five percent (25 percent) indicated that less than 40 percent of their undergraduate students were Catholic. Twenty-three percent (23 percent) stated that more than 60 percent of their undergraduate students were Catholic. Only 7 percent said they did not have this information.

Profile of Student Affairs

The largest student affairs staff numbered 430, and the smallest numbered three. However, while the number of student affairs professionals differed widely, depending on the size of the institution, the list of activities and services they provide their students did not. Clearly, student affairs professionals at small institutions wear many hats and play many roles. Just as clearly, senior student affairs officers head complex organizations regardless of the number of professionals they supervise.

The following offices or functions were cited by over 75 percent of the respondents: residence life (95 percent), student activities and organizations (93 percent), student conduct (92 percent), personal counseling (91 percent), housing operations [separate from residence life] (90 percent), alcohol and other drug programming (89 percent), leadership programming (89 percent), new student orientation (88 percent), and health center/services (85 percent).

At least 50 percent of the respondents supervise the following offices or functions: intramural sports (69 percent), multicultural affairs (69 percent), Title IX compliance [not athletics] (62 percent), career counseling (55 percent), and student center management (50 percent).

At least 25 percent cited LGBT services (49 percent), intercollegiate athletics (47 percent), public safety/campus police (44 percent), campus ministry (42 percent), community service (42 percent), food service liaison (39 percent), accessibility/disability support (37 percent), international student services (31 percent), Greek life (29 percent), and retention office/services (27 percent).

Other offices or functions that SSAOs supervised were academic advising (13 percent), study abroad (11 percent), financial aid (8 percent), and admission/enrollment management (7 percent). Individual responses also included alumni affairs, veterans' services, child care centers, commuter services, and TRIO programs.

The greatest change in the list was the addition of LGBT services by 49 percent of the respondents. These services were not mentioned in the previous surveys.

> "Clearly, student affairs professionals at small institutions wear many hats and play many roles."

Profile of the Senior Student Affairs Officer

Ninety-one percent (91 percent) of the respondents identified as white. Fifty-two percent (52 percent) identified as male, with 48 percent identifying as female. No one selected "other" as a response, although that was an alternative. Thirty-nine percent (39 percent) are between the ages of 51 and 60; 32 percent are between 41 and 50; 21 percent are 61 or older; and 8 percent are 40 or younger. Eighty percent (80 percent) are Catholic; 15 percent indicated a Protestant denomination; one indicated Muslim; and four respondents indicated no religion. Fifty-five percent (55 percent) have a Ph.D., Ed.D., or other terminal degree such as a J.D., while 43 percent indicated they have a master's degree. These percentages are substantially the same as the percentages reported in the 2005 survey. The greatest change is that in 2005, 12 percent of the respondents were priests, sisters, or brothers. That 2005 percentage decreased from the 23 percent in the 1996 survey. In the current survey, only 5 percent indicated that they were either a priest (4 percent) or sister (1 percent). These data clearly document the continuing decline of individuals in consecrated life in the role of the senior student affairs officer. They also indicate a continuing lack of diversity in the SSAO position.

There is evidence in this survey that the lay men and women who lead student affairs at Catholic colleges and universities are connected to discussions of Catholic identity. Ninety percent (90 percent) of the respondents were familiar with the *Principles of Good Practice for Student Affairs at Catholic Colleges and Universities*. Ninety-seven percent (97 percent) of those with familiarity said they use the Principles either often (36 percent) or sometimes (61 percent). Most respondents said that they or their staff members were involved in Catholic organizations such as ACCU (25 percent), ASACCU (46 percent), JASPA (18 percent), or other charism-based organizations (10 percent). Three respondents were involved in the Cardinal Newman Society.

EXPECTATIONS AND CONTRIBUTIONS

When asked what the SSAO expected from their staffs, the answers most often given were to respect the Catholic identity of the institution (48 percent) and to support the mission (34 percent). Only two respondents indicated that they expected the majority of the staff to be Catholic.

The SSAOs were asked to list the specific things that their divisions did to support the Catholic mission of the institution. The answers most often given were service trips and activities (15 percent), the activities of the campus ministry office (13 percent), special programming around dates significant to the sponsoring order (11 percent), and student life policies (9 percent), specifically residence hall visitation policies and speaker policies. Other responses include incorporating Catholic perspectives into student leadership programs (9 percent), student conduct hearings (7 percent), new student orientation (6 percent), learning communities (5 percent), and resident assistant training (2 percent).

ISSUES

Seventy-two (72) respondents answered the open-ended question, "What are the most important issues faced on your campus related to Catholic identity?" The following list is in descending order of frequency.

1. LGBTQ issues: 31 (43 percent). Seven respondents (10 percent) cited same-sex marriage specifically, including how their institution will address legally married same-sex couples in housing and benefits.

2. Catholic values regarding sexual behavior versus the dominant culture: 21 (29 percent)

3. Diverse student body and staff versus "being Catholic": 9 (12.5 percent)

4. (tie) Diminishing student faith, knowledge, and interest in religion and Finding and retaining staff who support the mission: 7 each (10 percent)

5. (tie) Catholic values versus academic freedom *and* Violence and incivility: 3 each (4 percent)

Other issues that were mentioned by at least one respondent were: decrease in presence of the sponsoring order, social justice issues, student mental health issues, and alcohol and other drug issues.

These responses indicate that student affairs professionals at Catholic colleges and universities address the same issues as their counterparts at secular institutions. It was interesting that few respondents cited racial justice as an aspect of Catholic identity or cited racial issues as something with which they struggled. Whether this is because of a lack of awareness, or is a result of a lack of diversity in the SSAO position, or is a response to how the open-ended questions were worded is unknown. However, what is clear is that respondents cite as their biggest issues those relating to the tension between traditional Catholic teaching and dominant American cultural values. It will surprise no one that the crucible of this tension is sexuality. This was true in the 1989 survey, the 1996 survey, and the 2005 survey.

GENDER IDENTITY

The biggest change in this survey was the emergence of LGBT issues as the number one answer. This finding clearly documents the emerging awareness of LGBT issues on our campuses. LGBT issues were not specifically addressed in the 1989 survey. In 1996, gay/lesbian issues ranked second to sexuality and sexual behavior as an important issue, although no exact number is cited in the published article. In 2005, 24 percent cited gay/lesbian issues as the third most frequent answer. Sexuality and sexual behavior was, again, first in that survey, with the religious diversity of staff and students cited second. It is important to note that these issues were framed in terms of *gay and lesbian; transgender* was not expressed. The current 2016 survey marks the emergence of an awareness of transgender identity and expresses the need to address the needs of transgender students for the first time.

CONCLUSION

The results of this survey confirm the belief that student affairs professionals at Catholic colleges and universities tackle some of the most difficult issues related to Catholic identity. The articles in this book provide the opportunity for these professionals to share their wisdom, experience, and good practices with one another.

Sandra M. Estanek is a professor of graduate education and leadership and director of the higher education and student affairs administration master's program at Canisius College in Buffalo, New York.

REFERENCES

Estanek, S. M. (2005). "Results of a Survey of Senior Student Affairs Officers at Catholic Colleges and Universities." *Current Issues in Catholic Higher Education* 24(2), 83-97.

Estanek, S. M. (1996). "A Study of Student Affairs Practice at Catholic Colleges and Universities." *Current Issues in Catholic Higher Education* 16(2), 63-72.

Riley, D. M. (1990). "ACCU Student Life Survey: A Report." *Current Issues in Catholic Higher Education* 10(2), 6-10.

CHAPTER 9

Getting Connected: Institutes, Organizations, and Opportunities

Alexandra Weber Bradley

Student affairs professionals at Catholic colleges and universities are hired for their professional competence but often arrive with little training in many aspects of the Catholic mission and may not have been educated at a Catholic institution (Estanek, Herdlein, & Harris, 2011; Renn & Jessup-Anger, 2008). Furthermore, many graduate programs in student affairs or higher education administration offer few occasions to learn about the unique opportunities and particularities of practicing student affairs at a Catholic college. Consequently, most colleges create orientation programs to build knowledge of the institutional mission and hire individuals who have an openness to integrate the values and mission of the college. New hires, as well as seasoned professionals, are encouraged to find a national community that provides training opportunities and dialogue on integrating Catholic mission and charism values into student affairs. Most find it helpful and life-giving to their career. This chapter will expand upon communities, institutes, and other opportunities for professional training at the national level.

THE ASSOCIATION FOR STUDENT AFFAIRS AT CATHOLIC COLLEGES AND UNIVERSITIES

The Association for Student Affairs at Catholic Colleges and Universities (ASACCU), founded in 1999, is the national professional organization for student affairs personnel working in Catholic higher education. The organization promotes the integration of the Catholic Intellectual Tradition into student affairs work. ASACCU strives to provide opportunities for cooperation, dialogue, and sharing of best practices among its members through its programming and activities. Catholic colleges are invited to join, as institutional members, with the membership being coordinated through the senior student affairs officer. ASACCU is affiliated with the Association of Catholic Colleges and Universities (ACCU), the national collective voice for Catholic higher education, which works to strengthen and promote the Catholic identity and university mission of its member campuses.

ASACCU hosts a conference each summer at a member campus, with the goals of sharing best practices and resources among colleagues while building a community "rooted in the highest standards of the profession and in the diversity of our gifts, stories, cultures, and faiths" (http://www.asaccu.org/index.php/purpose). The annual conference is open to student affairs professionals in Catholic higher education at all levels of their careers. For senior student affairs officers, ASACCU sponsors a roundtable event each fall. The one-day conference discusses important issues that the senior student affairs officers see arising on their campuses. ASACCU also promotes best practices and continuing education through its publications and awards, such as the Mission Integration Awards, the Founders' Award, and the Sandra M. Estanek, Ph.D. Young Alumni Award.

THE JESUIT ASSOCIATION OF STUDENT PERSONNEL ADMINISTRATORS (JASPA)

Although focused on student affairs professionals who work at the 28 Jesuit colleges and universities in the United States, JASPA was the first association to focus on the distinctiveness of practicing student affairs in Catholic higher education. JASPA was founded in 1954, although the first documented meeting of deans of men at Jesuit institutions occurred in 1936. JASPA sponsors several programs and services for its members, including an annual spring conference, a series of webinars, and networking opportunities for various functional areas in student life. Its publications, such as *The Ignatian Imperative: Student Affairs Educators in Jesuit Higher Education* (Thon, 2013), and its annual awards, such as the Rev. Victor R. Yanitelli, S.J. Award, the Ignatian Medal, the Outstanding Commitment to Diversity and Social Justice Award, and the JASPA Scholarship Award, highlight best practices at Jesuit institutions. Every five years, JASPA offers a summer institute for members to gather and reflect on their roles and commitment to educating the whole person.

An important publication sponsored by ASACCU, ACCU, and JASPA is the *Principles of Good Practice for Student Affairs at Catholic Colleges and Universities*. The document, published after several years of dialogue and consultation with Catholic campus professionals, outlines eight guiding principles and expectations of student affairs at a Catholic college. In addition, it includes diagnostic queries that campuses can use in discussing how to implement the principles at their college or university. Campuses can use the *Principles* as part of an effort to assess mission integration, in planning new programs or evaluating current services, or as a tool for staff development and student leader training.

An additional publication that can be used to spur conversation on Catholic identity in student affairs is ACCU's *Strengthening Catholic Identity* series. The 12-

part series addresses topics such as student affairs, spiritual and liturgical life, Catholic Social Teaching, and faith and reason. These publications can be helpful for student affairs professionals seeking to learn more about the integration of Catholic mission or to discuss with staff members in program evaluation, professional development, reading groups, or strategic planning.

INSTITUTES

ACCU sponsors several annual opportunities for student affairs professionals to learn more about Catholic higher education. For those in entry-level or mid-career positions, the Mission Integration Institute at the University of San Diego offers a four-day program focusing on the role of faith and spirituality in Catholic higher education. Sessions focus on student formation, faith, spirituality, Catholic Social Teaching, and integrating service and justice. Senior student affairs leaders from University of San Diego and other Catholic colleges serve as faculty at the Institute and lead participants in expanding their own personal understanding of faith and how to help students on their campuses grow in their spiritual lives.

Two additional programs co-sponsored by ACCU help senior-level student affairs officers learn more about Catholic mission. The annual Rome Seminar brings senior administrators from all areas of the university, faculty leaders, and trustees to Rome to learn more about the global Church and the Vatican. The Seminar includes meetings with members of the Curia, journalists, and representatives from Rome's pontifical universities. The Seminar also includes experiences that enable participants to reflect on their personal faith through visits to holy sites and a general audience with the Pope. Participants serve as ambassadors to Rome on behalf of their institutions, sharing best practices and success stories from their campuses with Curia officials to promote a mutual understanding of Catholic higher education in the United States.

Also aimed for senior administrators, the Institute for Administrators in Catholic Higher Education (IACHE) is a four-day summer seminar bringing together scholars and leaders at Catholic colleges and universities to address some of the most pressing issues facing campuses. The seminar, co-sponsored by Boston College and ACCU, is hosted on the Boston College campus each year. Hearing from top-level practitioners and Catholic higher education scholars, participants discuss the Catholic Intellectual Tradition, animating a life-giving Catholic culture, and best practices in mission assessment. Open to senior administrators from all areas of the university, the conversations are enriched by the diversity of participants and their experiences at Catholic colleges across the globe.

CHARISM-BASED ORGANIZATIONS

Most Catholic colleges in the United States were founded by religious congregations that emphasize particular values in their ministry (i.e., charism) and integrate these values into the specific mission of their colleges. The charism associations often offer opportunities for connecting with administrators at other colleges sponsored by the same religious order and to learn more about the charism values these institutional ministries share. For instance, the Lasallian Christian Brothers offer the Buttimer Institute of Lasallian Studies for leaders at colleges and universities founded by their congregation, involving intensive study of the Lasallian spiritual and educational mission and a practicum experience incorporating the skills learned through the program. The Lasallian Christian Brothers also offer the Brother John Johnston Institute of Contemporary Lasallian Practice; open to potential leaders to learn more about the Lasallian vision and educational mission, it concludes with a capstone portfolio project in which participants propose ways to integrate what they have learned into their current work.

For student affairs professionals at colleges and universities sponsored by the Benedictine order, the Benedictine Pedagogy Conference is a national opportunity to learn more about the 10 hallmarks of Benedictine education. Student affairs professionals are invited to attend the annual conference along with faculty and administrators to discuss how Benedictine values are incorporated into student life activities and into the classroom. The conference features opportunities to share best practices, participate in workshops, and network with colleagues from other Benedictine colleges.

At colleges sponsored by the Sisters of Mercy, the Conference for Mercy Higher Education (CMHE) plans programming focused on leadership development, Catholic identity, and Mercy mission, including a national biennial leadership formation program. CMHE also offers annual student programs in Washington, DC and at the United Nations, which student affairs professionals are encouraged to attend with their students.

The Association of Franciscan Colleges & Universities (AFCU) hosts a symposium, held at a member institution every other year, bringing together faculty, administrators, and staff to discuss Catholic identity and Franciscan mission. Breakout sessions focus on mission integration in various areas of the university, including enrollment, advancement, and student success and retention. These examples illustrate ways student affairs staff can learn more about the Catholic mission and charism values of their universities and make strong connections to others in the field.

Many opportunities for student affairs professionals to advance their knowledge and deepen their understanding of Catholic identity and university mission are available on a national level. Through membership in student affairs organizations and attendance at the institutes, conferences, and seminars offered, student affairs professionals can stay current and more effectively dialogue with their students on current issues in light of Catholic values.

Alexandra Weber Bradley is director of member services and programs at the Association of Catholic Colleges and Universities in Washington, DC.

REFERENCES

Estanek, S. M., Herdlein, R. & Harris, J. (2011). "Preparation of New Professionals and Mission-driven Hiring Practices: A Survey of Senior Student Affairs Officers at Catholic Colleges and Universities," *College Student Affairs Journal* 29(2), 151-163.

Renn, K. A. & Jessup-Anger, E. R. (2008). "Preparing New Professionals: Lessons for Graduate Preparation Programs from the National Study of New Professionals in Student Affairs," *Journal of College Student Development* 49(4), 319-335.

Thon, A. J. (2013). *The Ignatian Imperative: Student Affairs Educators in Jesuit Higher Education.* Milwaukee, WI: Marquette University.

SECTION THREE

Theoretical Perspectives

CHAPTER 10 The Living Tradition of *Ex corde Ecclesiae*   **61**
for Student Affairs

*Barbara Humphrey McCrabb,
United States Conference of Catholic Bishops*

CHAPTER 11 A Christian Anthropology for Student   **65**
Development

Michael J. James, Boston College

CHAPTER 12 Character Formation and Moral   **69**
Development: Creating an Intentional
Framework

Catherine WoodBrooks, Assumption College

CHAPTER 10

The Living Tradition of *Ex corde Ecclesiae* for Student Affairs

Barbara Humphrey McCrabb

Student affairs in Catholic higher education uniquely contributes to the university's identity, mission, and charism when it embodies the vision of *Ex corde Ecclesiae*.

FOUR DIMENSIONS

While the primary function of a Catholic college or university is education, the pursuit of truth, student affairs enriches the institutional endeavor by creating a learning environment in and out of the classroom. The way in which student affairs facilitates campus culture is distinct and complementary to the academic enterprise. Four dimensions illustrate the vital contributions that student affairs makes to the Catholic identity of the institution: a holistic pedagogy, an integrative approach, a healthy exploration, and Christian inspiration.

Using a *holistic pedagogy,* student affairs cultivates a vibrant community with a variety of co-curricular activities. A welcoming environment lays a foundation for relationships across academic disciplines and affinity groups. Community life thrives when rooted in respect, collaboration, and justice. Building on the intellectual pursuits of the students, effective student affairs speaks the language of the head, heart, and hands. In this dynamic environment where the arts and athletics abound, men and women hone their abilities and the human person flourishes.

Student affairs fosters opportunities for students to *integrate* personal beliefs, as well as religious and moral principles, with their academics and co-curricular activities. Students apply what they have learned to their lived experience and to real-world situations. They test theories within the campus environment and beyond. The value of integration both supports and challenges students, faculty, and administrators to be clear about the ramifications of its "talk" and the demands of its "walk." Integration leads to an appreciation of the genuine harmony between faith and reason.

Healthy exploration speaks to the inviting, creative, and diverse environment of the college campus. Through a variety of culture, service, art, and athletic activities,

> "Student life thrives at the crossroads where students, faculty, and staff can genuinely encounter Jesus in and through one another."

students can try new adventures or deepen their understanding of a current interest as they mature and grow intellectually, emotionally, and spiritually. In this environment, students discover positive ways to cross cultural and religious barriers. They consider the challenges of the common good and the need for justice.

While the first three dimensions could be true of other institutions of higher education, the fourth dimension — *Christian inspiration* — grounds a Catholic university in the rich tradition of faith. Student affairs at a Catholic institution is rooted in a "Christian anthropology, founded on the person of Christ, which will bring the dynamism of the creation and redemption to bear on reality" (ECE 33). Christian principles, such as human dignity and the need for community, are fundamental goals of student affairs. Therefore, student life thrives at the crossroads where students, faculty, and staff can genuinely encounter Jesus in and through one another.

EX CORDE ECCLESIAE

These four dimensions of student affairs in a Catholic university are inspired by *Ex corde Ecclesiae*, an apostolic exhortation (1990), which provides a universal vision for Catholic higher education. This exhortation addresses the identity and mission that Saint John Paul II articulated as four characteristics: "(1) a Christian inspiration not only of individuals but of the university community as such; (2) a continuing reflection in the light of the Catholic faith upon the growing treasury of human knowledge, to which it seeks to contribute by its own research; (3) fidelity to the Christian message as it comes to us through the Church; (4) an institutional commitment to the service of the people of God and of the human family in their pilgrimage to the transcendent goal which gives meaning to life."

Certain aspects of *Ex corde Ecclesiae* underscore the importance of student affairs. The primacy of person (ECE 18) means meeting students where they are and helping them grow and develop, not only intellectually but as a whole person. The synthesis (ECE 19) of knowledge seeks to integrate faith and reason, relying upon a high degree of self-awareness and openness to the other. The cultivation of freedom, charity, respect, dialogue, and protection of individual rights (ECE 21) are foundational to the work of student affairs. The Church in dialogue with culture borrows elements from the culture to proclaim the Gospel effectively to each generation (ECE 43-47).

THE U.S. APPLICATION

In *The Application of Ex corde Ecclesiae for the United States*, the bishops offered practical guidance to Catholic colleges and universities within our national context. After affirming the four distinctive characteristics, the bishops articulated expectations and described a series of commitments, several of which apply to student affairs: first, the commitment to Catholic ideals, principles, and attitudes in carrying out research, teaching, and all other university activities; second, the commitment to witness the Catholic faith by Catholic administrators and teachers… as well as acknowledgement and respect (of the faith) on the part of non-Catholic teachers and administrators; and finally, the commitment to create a campus culture and environment that is expressive and supportive of a Catholic way of life (U.S. App Pt I, 7).

Faculty and administrators are asked not only to model Catholic ideals, but also to be witnesses. It was Pope Paul VI who said that people listen to a witness. If they (students) listen to teachers, it is because they are also witnesses. To be a witness requires a certain integrity and harmony in one's actions and beliefs in light of the Gospel.

In 2011, the U.S. bishops conducted a ten-year review of the implementation of *The Application of Ex corde Ecclesiae for the United States*. The review acknowledged progress and highlighted a clear path forward. The review identified several strategic topics: advancing Catholic identity through continued dialogue between bishops and presidents; hiring for mission; forming faculty, staff, and trustees in Catholic identity; and the need to improve students' theological and catechetical knowledge.

WORLD CONGRESS ON CATHOLIC EDUCATION

In 2015, the Congregation for Catholic Education in Rome celebrated 25 years of *Ex corde Ecclesiae*. The World Congress highlighted the firm link between the identity of education institutions and their mission, which flows from the very identity of the Church. *Ex corde Ecclesiae* literally means "from the heart of the Church." The Church claims Catholic education as part of the Church's mission to evangelize the world. The Church entrusts the educating community with the care and guidance of evangelization. Catholic educators share a common bond in their mission to form and educate according to a Catholic vision.

At the conference, Pope Francis reflected on the challenges of our day: the need for holistic education, the ability to create new pathways, and the concern for those on the peripheries. Education in a Christian manner introduces the learner to the whole truth, leading people forward in human values toward transcendence. Academia cultivates the intellectual life, learning primarily with the head. Student affairs promotes learning through the heart and hands utilizing relationships, art, play, and experience. Pope Francis encouraged Catholic educators to take reasonable risk. Like learning to walk, the skill of balancing the tension between what is known and unknown keeps us stable and open to new possibilities. He argued that new pathways require creativity. What if a fresh perspective on cooperation across disciplines, beyond the usual suspects, led to discovery? How can modern technology make learning more accessible?

Pope Francis invited educators to go to the peripheries and to "make (students) grow in humanity, in intelligence, in values, and in attitudes so that they can go forward, bringing to others experiences they do not know." For those on the margins, their experience of survival, cruelty, hunger, and injustice reflect their wounded humanity. Yet our salvation comes from the wounds of an innocent man who died on the cross for us. Good pedagogy allows those on the margins to draw wisdom from their wounds and offers a way forward. "The greatest failure an educator can have is to educate … within a selective community, a culture of security, or an affluent social group. When we stay within the walls, we no longer move forward."

CONCLUSION

I am reminded of a passage from the prophet Micah: "You have been told, O mortal, what is good, and what the Lord requires of you: Only to act justly, to love tenderly, and to walk humbly with your God" (6:8).

This passage offers wise counsel to those of us in student affairs. The call to love is embodied in the concern for the whole person, a person in community, and a person for others. Justice roots the human person in right relationship that the four dimensions of student affairs address. Finally, walking humbly with God grounds this perspective on student affairs at a Catholic university or college in a Christian anthropology that sees human flourishing as possible only when God, the transcendent, is encountered in the human horizon — not as a concept or a power — but as a person.

Barbara Humphrey McCrabb is the assistant director for higher education at the United States Conference of Catholic Bishops in Washington, DC.

CHAPTER 11

A Christian Anthropology for Student Development

Michael J. James

WHERE IS THE LOVE?

Since the spring semester of 2014, I have offered an upper-level undergraduate course titled, "Spirituality, Religion, and the College Student Experience." The 30 to 35 juniors and seniors enrolled in the course represent majors from across the university with gender, ethnicity, and religious affiliation reflecting the broader student body at the university. The course addresses themes from ecumenical and interreligious perspectives and aims to understand the dynamics of faith life and spiritual life for students as they navigate their identity in the context of contemporary academic culture.

One of, if not, *the* most provocative insights with which a student illuminated my class came in the form of a sincere question. We reached the mid-semester point. I devoted the beginning of a class to assess students' quality of engagement and satisfaction with the course. In response, students offered a list of topics, readings, discussion themes, and group project feedback that struck them as interesting, challenging, or at least memorable. Amid the litany of secularization narratives, sociology of religion statistics, student development theories, and descriptive characteristics of contemporary higher education, one student raised her hand, stood up and asked *the* question, "Where is the love?"

As faculty members and administrators, we are challenged every day to respond authentically — with humility and reverence — to my student's question, "Where is the love?" As educators, we recognize that the task of becoming human is a lifelong project. Education, at every level, must be devoted to contributing something meaningful to the task of becoming fully human. As educators at Catholic colleges and universities, our work — our vocation — is informed by a tradition whose wisdom asserts that the education of the person is the education of the *whole* person. Ideally, as members of Catholic colleges and universities, we accept the responsibilities of fostering genuine community, of creating environments that demand cooperation and mutual support,

> "The question (one that I am convinced is on the minds and in the hearts of all our students) is, 'Do you love me?'"

of providing opportunities for all members of the community to be served and in turn serve those in most need, and of engaging in critical reflection on the prevailing cultural values that potentially contribute to the common good, or damage the human condition.

DO YOU LOVE ME?

I believe that my student's question, "Where is the love?" was a safe way of asking a deeper, riskier question — one with greater personal moral agency. The question (one that I am convinced is on the minds and in the hearts of all our students) is, "Do you love me?" This is a question that we cannot afford to dismiss. Our response indicates one dimension of how we "form individual students." If we respond authentically to the question, "Do you love me?" our goal really becomes to form individual students to recognize God-Love within themselves. The twin goals of Catholic colleges and universities to form individual students and to build the community become, to a certain extent, both the method and the consequence of a community that is discovering God-Love. In this way, we become more fully human.

THE ART OF LOVING

At the end of the semester, a student came to see me in my office to discuss her future goals. After describing to me her plan to spend a year of service followed by medical school, she declared, "You are the only professor in four years to tell me that you love me." I looked at her with a combination of feelings of both surprise and self-consciousness. Before I could respond, she leaned in and asked in a hushed voice, "Do other faculty and staff love me?" I confidently responded that when a professor comes to class prepared and enthusiastic about the course theme and content, she is telling you that she loves you. When a career services counselor spends hours reading and evaluating your résumés and cover letters with thorough and constructive feedback, he is telling you that he loves you. When a residence hall director patiently and empathetically listens to the description of your roommate selection anxiety, she is telling you that she loves you. When the student activities staff spends time beyond normal office hours reviewing and crafting an equitable response to your student club's request for additional resources, they are telling you that they love you. "Yes," I said. Although we may not say the words often, or at all, administrators, faculty, and staff have been telling you for four years that they love you.

My conversation with this student reminded me of the sacramental opportunity we are invited into through our mission. Catholic colleges and universities offer a distinct, formative, and transformative student development experience — the kind of experience that is animated by the life of Jesus. A Christian anthropology for student development calls us to encounter Jesus in one another through love. As student affairs professionals at Catholic colleges and universities, we are called to live a vocation that invites all members of the community to practice the "art of loving."

The "art of loving" is demanding. It requires us to *love everyone* — acknowledging that our dignity and value are not external, but inherent; not dependent on what we do, but who we are: made in the image of God, the *Imago Dei*. It is selfless. It calls us to *share the joy and pain of another person* by letting go of our own strong beliefs, opinions, and ideas in order to make the other's perspective our own. It is generous. We are asked to *be the first to love* in each encounter. We ask ourselves, "What is the will of God in this moment, with this person?" The answer is simple: to love that person who is made in the image of God. We must initiate love for the other right away without expecting anything in return. It is reciprocal. We come to understand, through the example of Jesus, that a person discovers his or her deepest, most authentic self by *being detached from the self*. To enter into relationship, we must identify and embrace our own self-identity, while at the same time relinquishing it for the sake of the other. Jesus shows us through His ultimate sacrifice that I am myself, not when I close myself off from the other, but when I give myself, when out of love I lose myself in the other. In this way, I actually find myself.

In his 2009 encyclical, *Caritas in Veritate*, Benedict XVI describes how the dynamic of personal relationships can be "illuminated in a striking way by the relationship of the Person of the Trinity within the one divine Substance." The pope emeritus explains, "God desires to incorporate us into the reality of this communion as well: 'that they may be one even as we are one' (Jn 17:22)." In this light, we understand that "true openness does not mean loss of individual identity but profound interpenetration" (54).

In the face of a secularist academic climate and on campuses that are too often marked by isolation, fragmentation, discontinuity, competition, and abject individualism, *our* practice in the "Art of Loving" will generate countercurrents of interdependence, relational action, dialogue, and reciprocity.

Michael J. James is a lecturer in the Department of Educational Leadership and Higher Education at Boston College and director of the Institute for Administrators in Catholic Higher Education.

REFERENCE

Benedict XVI. (2009). "*Caritas in Veritate:* On Integral Human Development in Charity and Truth." Retrieved from http://w2.vatican.va/content/benedict-xvi/en/encyclicals/documents/hf_ben-xvi_enc_20090629_caritas-in-veritate.html.

CHAPTER 12

Character Formation and Moral Development: Creating an Intentional Framework

Catherine WoodBrooks

Catholic colleges and universities, like all faith-based institutions, measure success largely by how well they instill moral, ethical, and spiritual growth in their students. Prospective students and their parents seem to concur; they cite the Catholic mission of character formation when seeking the right institutional fit. But how can we guarantee that our graduating students will have grown morally and spiritually? How do we measure character? In this chapter, I will describe a research project that led me to think more strategically about how to offer and assess strategies for students' moral, ethical, and spiritual growth.

Claims regarding educational learning outcomes are usually distributed among three general categories: knowledge; skills; and dispositions, which is a term for values or attitudes. Undergraduate institutions often translate dispositions as a result of a holistic education that prepares students to grasp concepts such as civic responsibility, philanthropy, and political activism. This preparation often takes the form of service-learning courses that apply theory to practice, giving students a firsthand look at social inequity, thereby igniting the social-justice spark. Similarly, colleges preparing future healthcare professionals anchor their curriculum in a code of ethics that permeates coursework, practicums, and internships.

Faith-based colleges and universities, however, confront a unique assessment challenge. Character formation, as we define it, is different from social awareness or medical ethics. It is steeped in a moral code directly connected to faith. Like faith, character is difficult to define.

NURTURING A CULTURE OF CHARACTER FORMATION

In 2007, through the generosity of the Teagle Foundation, three Catholic colleges embarked on a four-year study that sought to measure students' moral, ethical, religious, and spiritual growth. Our proposed learning goal was both simple and challenging: When confronted with life choices, students would consider ethical, moral, and religious perspectives espoused by the college as well as other traditions, and their actions would be founded on respect for the dignity of the human person. Though not a description of the full study, results showed that seniors demonstrated a modest improvement over first-year students in making value-based choices. We assessed character growth through traditional means, e.g., surveys and a direct-assessment tool that used a rubric for faculty observation of students wrestling with a moral dilemma. It was in student focus groups, however, that we unearthed the largest amount of significant information.

STRATEGY ONE: CREATE OPPORTUNITIES

Participants in all focus groups from the three campuses agreed that the colleges provide opportunities that foster moral and spiritual growth. The overall attitude toward these opportunities was positive: Students were grateful for the emphasis on the "whole student." The first-year students identified separation from parents and increased independence as necessary for their moral and spiritual growth. They felt this separation would force them to clarify their own values. Most students expressed having "fixed" values prior to college, due to the strong influence of their parents. However, a universal belief among the first-year students was that interacting with peers would help them solidify their values and beliefs. Specifically, they were looking to better understand their own character through meeting peers with values both like and different from their own.

In contrast to first-year students, fourth-year students identified formal academic and co-curricular activities as the more influential means by which their respective colleges supported students' moral and spiritual growth. They listed courses, retreats, leadership training, and service experiences as elements that helped clarify their values. Although they discussed features of "the college experience" as contributing to their own character development, they more frequently mentioned supportive faculty and staff who had taken a personal interest in them.

STRATEGY TWO: IDENTIFY BARRIERS AND POSSIBLE INCENTIVES TO INCREASE PARTICIPATION

Our focus groups pointed out barriers that prevent students from accessing character-building activities and programs that our campuses make available. More often than not, students mentioned a hesitation of attending anything that sounded too "religious." Others viewed participation as problematic, or even impossible, primarily because of other overwhelming demands on their time. There is an irony here, of course. Reflection is a key component in Catholic teaching, yet our students' increasingly hectic schedules discourage quiet time for individual reflection and thoughtful discussion.

Our results suggest two options worth exploring to increase participation. *First*, tap into the remarkable power of peer influence. First-year students are attracted to activities that create social links with fellow students. Seniors report that an invitation from a member of a well-established network of friends is the single most likely factor to persuade them to pursue an interest. Both class years stated that one sometimes participated in an activity simply because of an invitation from a close friend. *Second*, design programs to be interactive. In nearly every focus group, students expressed a strong desire to both listen to others' opinions and express their own when it came to making intentional, moral choices. Seniors particularly relished opportunities to discuss and debate hotly contested moral issues (e.g., assisted suicide, abortion, gender reassignment surgery) inside and outside the classroom.

> "Reflection is a key component in Catholic teaching, yet our students' increasingly hectic schedules discourage quiet time."

The Teagle study confirmed that students are greatly influenced by their peers and that they want to engage, either formally or informally, in value-laden discussions. The question then becomes how we frame those discussions to promote moral and spiritual growth and reflection.

Because peer acceptance is so important to students, they may hesitate to offer an opinion that diverges from the majority. One way to mitigate this problem is to use polling technology. After a presentation and prior to a large group discussion, students use their smartphones to anonymously choose a response from a set of questions that most resembles their opinion about the discussion topic. When they view a graph depicting the range of responses and see that they are not alone in their opinion, they may be less reluctant to share theirs with the group. The program becomes more interesting if the technology allows students to change their minds and select another answer when they are influenced by a comment interjected by the discussion facilitator or a peer during the discussion. This polling technique, accessed by a variety of integrated software tools, offers an instant assessment of how engaged students are in the discussion and how they are influenced by others' opinions.

We also discovered that students claim to be heavily influenced by caring faculty and staff. The worth of strong alliances between student affairs and faculty cannot be overstated. For instance, we know that students who participate in retreats often describe them as transformative, yet many students are reluctant to carve time out from their busy schedules to do so. Faculty who oversee honors or first-year programs may welcome the chance to partner with student affairs on a retreat designed specifically for their students.

STRATEGY THREE: MENTORING

James Keenan, SJ, (2004) offers great insight for student affairs professionals when he reminds us that the call to be a Christian is a call to grow in love, a "summons" to pursue the right way for growing. Catholic higher education is distinctive in its capacity to create a mentoring environment. We initiate authentic relationships with students by first demonstrating our commitment to them, and that commitment often begins with listening — in focus groups, in classrooms, and in one-to-one encounters. When we establish mutual trust with our students, meaningful conversations naturally emerge.

We are reminded throughout the Gospels of the importance of the relationship between elders and young people. The role we take on as mentors within the context of our students' faith journeys, therefore, should be undertaken with a great deal of thoughtful contemplation. As we are called to be a witness to our faith in the goodness of God, in His glorious nature and character, we must also be aware of how we are responding to our own inevitable work struggles. In short, be aware that our students are watching us — and they notice everything. How many times do our graduates fondly recall something we have said or done that profoundly influenced their way of thinking?

Perhaps the most important thing we can share during some of those heart-to-hearts with students is the beauty of God's grace, mercy, and forgiveness. His unconditional love is a difficult concept for people to accept. We strive to be our best possible selves, but God still loves us even at our worst. The more intentional we are about living virtuous lives, however, the less likely we are to fall into ungodliness. Aristotle calls this habitual formation of character its "second nature," one that closely unites the soul to the human being. Our capacity to help students wrestle with moral challenges is immense, and in so doing, we hope to nurture that seamless connection between moral thought and moral action.

Catherine WoodBrooks is the vice president for student affairs at Assumption College in Worcester, Massachusetts.

REFERENCES

Austin, T., Lau, A., & WoodBrooks, C. (2012). "Assessing Students' Moral and Spiritual Growth at Catholic Liberal Arts Colleges: A Collaborative Grant-funded Initiative," *Journal of College Student Values* 13(4), 1-8.

Keenan, J. F. (2004). *Moral Wisdom: Lessons Learned and Texts from the Catholic Tradition.* Lanham, MD: Rowman & Littlefield.

SECTION FOUR

Practical Applications

PRINCIPLE ONE: 77
*Welcomes all students into a vibrant community that
celebrates God's love for all.*

PRINCIPLE TWO: 101
*Grounds policies, practices, and decisions in the teachings and
living tradition of the Church. Builds and prepares the student
affairs staff to make informed contributions to the Catholic
mission of the institution.*

PRINCIPLE THREE: 121
*Enriches student integration of faith and reason through
provision of co-curricular learning opportunities.*

PRINCIPLE FOUR: 137
*Creates opportunities for students to experience, reflect upon,
and act from a commitment to justice, mercy, and compassion,
and in light of Catholic social teaching to develop respect and
responsibility for all, especially those most in need.*

PRINCIPLE FIVE: 149
*Challenges students to high standards of personal behavior and
responsibility through the formation of character and virtues.*

PRINCIPLE SIX: 167
*Invites and accompanies students into the life of the Catholic
Church through prayer, liturgy, sacraments, and spiritual direction.*

PRINCIPLE SEVEN: 177
*Seeks dialogue among religious traditions and with
contemporary culture to clarify beliefs and to foster mutual
understanding in the midst of tensions and ambiguities.*

PRINCIPLE EIGHT: 189
*Assists students in discerning and responding to their vocations,
understanding potential professional contributions, and
choosing particular career directions.*

PRINCIPLE ONE

Welcomes all students into a vibrant community that celebrates God's love for all.

CHAPTER 13 Catholic Hospitality: The Foundation for   79
Community in Catholic Higher Education

Lisa L. Kirkpatrick, St. Edward's University

CHAPTER 14 Faith Matters: Supporting Students'   83
Religious Diversity

Kristine Cyr Goodwin, Providence College

CHAPTER 15 Race and Social Justice: Lessons from   89
Ferguson and St. Louis University

*Mona Hicks and Kent Porterfield,
Saint Louis University*

CHAPTER 16 Walking the Two-Way Bridge: Transgender   95
at Catholic Colleges and Universities

Sandra M. Estanek, Canisius College

CHAPTER 13

Catholic Hospitality: The Foundation for Community in Catholic Higher Education

Lisa L. Kirkpatrick

Catholic higher education is a distinctive learning experience and environment in which we have the opportunity to take Catholic teachings well beyond traditional educational spaces. In addition, our campuses resemble microcosms of our larger communities and they become practice fields for our students as they transform in "real time" into advanced versions of themselves, preparing to take on the challenges of our world. We are called to embrace each of our students as they are — realizing that their next several years of exploration is our invitation to journey with them, in practice and preparation, for what is to come. It is our responsibility to inspire, imagine, and foster the "big questions and worthy dreams" (Parks, 2011, p. 240-241) of our students through the community life we build on our campuses. What positions Catholic higher education so well to do this is that we can ground the work of student affairs in the tradition of Christian/Catholic hospitality. Hospitality is one of the oldest and most critical Christian virtues and can be understood as welcoming, caring for, and engaging "the other," not just the powerful, but strangers and those at the margins as well (Pohl, 1999; Vogt, 2007; Wrobleski, 2012).

Modeling Catholic hospitality throughout the college experience supports student preparation and teaches students the habits of thinking, feeling, and acting that bring about social justice and God's fierce and unending love for all, as lived and expressed through one another. From a student development perspective, while discussing the transformation and maturity of the college student in faith, Parks (2011) states that the student's transformation is dependent upon "the hospitality, aspirations, and commitment of adult culture as mediated through both individuals and institutions" (p. 10). Grounding our work as student affairs professionals in the tradition of Catholic hospitality strengthens our ability to affect student success and the student experience.

Furthermore, a study done at UCLA's Higher Education Research Institute (Astin, Astin, & Lindholm, 2011) looked at how to assess spiritual and religious qualities of college students and the role college plays in their development.

The spiritual and religious qualities described in the study were of interest because:

> ... *technical knowledge alone will not be adequate for dealing with some of society's most pressing problems: violence, poverty, crime, divorce, substance abuse, and the religious, national, and ethnic conflicts that continue to plague our country and our world. At root, these are problems of the spirit, problems that call for greater self-awareness, self-understanding, equanimity, empathy, and concern for others.* (Astin, Astin, & Lindholm, 2011, p. 8).

Catholic hospitality helps foster these characteristics in our students and is an integral part of our greater mission as Catholic colleges and universities and extensions of the Catholic Church. Similarly, Eboo Patel (2012) writes of prejudice, war, and poverty at least partially as a result of religious illiteracy and the fear of difference, as well as the inability to engage in healthy interfaith dialogue. Teaching our students to embrace the world and its differences, within a framework of hospitality, can contribute to a greater global understanding and ethic of care.

Catholic hospitality is demonstrated in a range of ways on our campuses today. Consider our extensive orientation and welcome programs that transition new students and families to our communities, helping them develop an appreciation for our mission as well as immediately feel that they belong and can thrive, even if they feel different or alone at first — an expression of universal love. Our intentionality surrounding campus rituals and traditions are meant to express openness, inclusion, humility, dignity, compassion, forgiveness, love, and gratitude. Student leaders are trained to connect with one another and their peers in ways that value the dignity of each person — even within conflict and disagreement; and student organizations work to foster self-understanding and purpose while probing and exploring others' cultures and supporting difference. Caring bystanders — more and more of our students — speak out and do something when someone is in danger. The motivation and the specific approaches we take are rooted in Catholic hospitality and demand that we work at being in right relationship with one another within the context of community, open to the encounter and exchange of guest and host, and experiencing one another as an expression of God's love.

These actions reflect habits and a disposition of Catholic hospitality embedded in our communities that demand constant attention and intentionality. Love in action is difficult work. Student affairs staff must champion the development of community on our campuses and collaborate broadly and deeply with faculty, staff, administration, and students to invigorate and support an inclusive community.

Student affairs practitioners can model the way, fostering Catholic hospitality with students. It is imperative that student affairs practitioners, including Catholic and non-Catholics, believers and non-believers, take responsibility for living the Catholic mission and ensuring that it infiltrates our campus communities. It is from a humble position that student affairs practitioners operate. It is not "for students," but "with students." It is from that same space of humility that collaboration with faculty may emerge as well. Ultimately, the work of Catholic hospitality is accomplished when it emanates from our students and is sustained by all of us.

> "It is from a humble position that student affairs practitioners operate."

Staff members do not necessarily arrive on our Catholic campuses prepared to do their work in a Catholic education context. They require preparation and supervision that empowers them to live the Catholic mission and to incorporate it into the daily acts of community building. Moreover, staff cannot be expected immediately and easily to see their work as sacramental. Narloch (2014) reminds us that the sacramental vision of Catholicism is "that each person is a manifestation of God's love" (p. 24) and that we present that through our work in service of students, families, and colleagues on our campuses, engaging the stranger and those we already know "as if they were Christ and treat them accordingly" (p. 24). Whether a believer or not, this understanding can be cultivated by leaders on campus who strive to serve students while modeling Jesus's love and the greater Catholic worldview.

Coaching student affairs practitioners to sustain a culture of Catholic hospitality begins with training and development opportunities to increase knowledge, application, synthesis, and good judgment about Catholic Church teachings as they relate to mission, the founding order, social justice, student faith and spiritual development, and moral reasoning. It is necessary to apply a common language for student affairs practitioners in order to create a common understanding about what it means to serve at a Catholic institution of higher education, from which to practice, reflect, and learn. It is only then that we can fully engage, with some level of competency and confidence, in sustaining Catholic hospitality in service of students.

It can also be the case that, when student affairs staff begin to engage in staff development with the intention of integrating Catholic tradition and mission, faculty become energized and interested, too. There is an organic, transformative effect on the culture of the campus — ideally a community of Catholic hospitality, grounded in

Catholic tradition. Promoting "safe and brave" space for staff, as well as the rest of the campus community, to wrestle through the difficult postmodern cultural challenges of student life — where the Catholic Church knowingly moves counter to prevailing societal attitudes — is another important idea to cultivate. Making Catholic Church teachings relevant in this day and age for our students is part of what me must all facilitate, translate, and communicate.

Catholic hospitality fosters personal responsibility and empowers all members of Catholic higher education communities to take responsibility for learning, living, and connecting with others for the greater good. A culture of Catholic hospitality on our campuses inspires power and agency in all individuals to manifest Catholic traditions and values. Our students, as future leaders, must take those Catholic traditions and values useful to the greater society into nontraditional spaces for the good of the world.

Lisa L. Kirkpatrick is vice president for student affairs and Title IX coordinator at St. Edward's University in Austin, Texas.

REFERENCES

Astin, A. W., Astin, H. S., & Lindholm, J. A. (2011). *Cultivating the Spirit: How College Can Enhance Students' Inner Lives*. San Francisco, CA: Jossey-Bass.

Hagstrom, A. A. (2013). "The Role of Charism and Hospitality in the Academy." *Integritas* 1(1), 1-14. doi: 10.6017/integritas.v1i1p1.

Narloch, R. (2014). "Cultivating Sacramentality Through Administrative Work: Guidance from St. Benedict on Being a Catholic Department Chair." *Journal of Catholic Higher Education* 33(1), 21-31.

Parks, S. D. (2011). *Big Questions, Worthy Dreams: Mentoring Emerging Adults in Their Search for Meaning, Purpose, and Faith.* San Francisco, CA: Jossey-Bass.

Patel, Eboo. (2012). *Sacred Ground: Pluralism, Prejudice, and the Promise of America.* Boston, MA: Beacon Press.

Pohl, C. D. (1999). *Making Room: Recovering Hospitality as a Christian Tradition.* Grand Rapids, MI: William B. Eerdmans Publishing Company.

Vogt, C. (2007). "Fostering a Catholic Commitment to the Common Good: An Approach Rooted in Virtue Ethics." *Theological Studies* 68, 394-417.

Wrobleski, J. (2012). *The Limits of Hospitality*. Collegeville, MN: Liturgical Press.

CHAPTER 14

Faith Matters: Supporting Students' Religious Diversity

Kristine Cyr Goodwin

Pope Francis (2016) refers to the need for a "culture of encounter," a culture that requires Christians to "go beyond the boundaries of their lives and encounter other people ... [This is] necessary for the healthy functioning in society." As student affairs practitioners, we are positioned to support students' faith development while helping them become more familiar with religions different from their own and to answer the call to develop a "culture of encounter" on our campuses.

Eboo Patel, founder of Interfaith Youth Core, challenges all colleges and universities that lay claim to preparing students for global citizenship to take religious diversity seriously (Patel, 2007). Providence College, where I serve as vice president, hosted the 2015 annual ASACCU conference. Its theme, *Widening Our Embrace: Inclusive Excellence through Hospitality, Solidarity, and Love,* touched upon key components for encouraging meaningful interfaith encounters. The theme also offered insight into how we may better engage students who do not identify with any religion.

In this chapter, I propose and support the belief that ecumenical and inter-religious/interfaith dialogue will move us closer to full realization of Principle One, which asks us to welcome all students into a vibrant campus community that celebrates God's love for all. After each section, I pose questions that may help readers reflect specifically on ways to put the themes of hospitality, solidarity, and love into practice.

HOSPITALITY

We know through the readings of Genesis that God was the ultimate host, creating a world abundant with beauty and natural riches for our pleasure. He gave us one another for companionship and friendship and called us to love one another as He loves us. It is in this context theme that hospitality should be considered.

Catholic colleges and universities must go beyond simply welcoming students. Hospitality is much, much more. Jesus, the ideal host according to Hellwig (1999), acts "invitationally" and we are called to do the same. True hospitality involves thoughtful, intentional discipline in which the other takes precedence over self. Assessment methods like surveys and focus groups may help reveal to us the extent to which students experience a sense of belonging, but we should never underestimate surprise encounters. For example, an orientation leader once informed me that one of our new students had not eaten dinner because the dining hall closed before sunset. It was Ramadan, a Muslim holy time that we had not considered in our planning. Allowing this student to practice her faith while living on campus is the very embodiment of hospitality, but we had somehow missed it. Whatever our students' faith practices may or may not be, we are called to welcome them with respect, for every person has value and is made in the image and likeness of God.

In a recent issue of *America* magazine, Saadia Ahmad (2016) wrote poignantly of her experience: "We are able to borrow traditions from other religions without compromising our own. This insight defined my interfaith journey as a Muslim at a Catholic college." I had the pleasure of knowing Saadia when she was a student at Providence College. Encountering Muslim students' fasting practices during Ramadan led me to increased adherence to, and understanding of, fasting as a Catholic, a practice I had undertaken as *pro forma*.

REFLECTION QUESTIONS:

- Do we consider religious holidays and observances in our planning?

- Have we asked students what it is like to be a student at a Catholic college and listened to their responses?

- To what extent do we regularly evaluate our programs, policies, services, and information materials using different religious lenses?

- How might we create encounters through which we learn about our own religious beliefs and traditions and better understand those of others?

SOLIDARITY

Solidarity is the remedy to the negative consequences of assimilation. I grew up in Lowell, Massachusetts, a city built on textile mills and factories. People frequently refer to my hometown, made up largely of immigrants, as a "melting pot." We had a small café bearing that name. I remember being offended by this reference, wondering why people would want to or, worse, be expected to "melt" or assimilate in order to belong. Solidarity, on the other hand, is defined as "unity among individuals with common interests." Synonyms include *cohesion, accord,* and *cooperation.* I often imagined Lowell as a kaleidoscope in which all the parts retained their size, shape, color, and being and that with the light of God a beautiful image is made.

At colleges and universities everywhere, the student body is eclectic: Catholics, evangelicals, Protestants, non-denominational Christians, Jews, Muslims, Buddhists, Hindus, agnostics, and more. I once asked my Muslim brother-in-law why he'd chosen to attend a Catholic college. Without hesitation, he said he wanted to be educated in a place where faith mattered. That has been my mantra ever since: *faith matters.* According to surveys distributed by the Higher Education Research Institute (HERI), only 15 percent of college students in the United States reported having no interest in religious or spiritual matters. The large majority of students who are at least seeking a stronger spiritual identity offers encouragement to those of us committed to this work. Regular and robust interfaith and ecumenical group discussions in residence halls, dining rooms, and classrooms aimed at understanding our own and others' values, beliefs, and religious traditions are not only essential for our campuses, but also for the world at large. The gift we bring by embracing Catholic Social Teaching on solidarity is the gift we also receive. We come to know others in deep and meaningful ways, which allows us to reflect more profoundly on our own faith tradition — and we all grow in the process.

Being in solidarity with another person or group requires that we communicate, in word and action, that we are in this together, that we are equal, and that we both expect to be changed by our encounter. It does not require the other person or group to give up who they are for the sake of belonging. And not only will we become wiser, we will become more compassionate, more loving. We will become a more sincere reflection of God in the world.

REFLECTION QUESTIONS:

- What, if anything, do students feel they have to give up to experience belonging on campus?

- To what extent do we, as a community, engage in regular and robust interfaith dialogues?

- How comfortable am I, my colleagues, and our students in participating in these conversations?

- How do we, as practitioners at Catholic colleges, foster ongoing and intentional opportunities for students to talk about religion and faith, or do we assume this happens organically because we are a Catholic institution?

> "We are called to, as St. Thomas Aquinas wrote, 'will the good of the other.'"

LOVE

In 1965, Pope Paul VI spoke of the need to reach out in love with other religions to find fertile ground where moral and spiritual goodness will grow. Good judgement and love, as universal values, are foundational to most, if not all, religions and necessary for individuals and communities to flourish. Fifty years later, Pope Francis also speaks of love in the context of knowing with certainty that, regardless of religious differences, we are all children of God.

When student affairs professionals are asked why they chose the profession, they often respond, "Because I love students." There is no denying that the work we do and the strong relationships we develop with students are often filled with feelings of deep affection. However, the love referenced above is longer lasting and less conditional than affection. It is a willful love. It is choosing to love as God commands us, demonstrating a commitment to each person equally and treating every person with respect and thoughtfulness, regardless of their beliefs or behaviors. We are called to, as St. Thomas Aquinas wrote, "will the good of the other." When this kind of love manifests in our work with students, we give witness to the goodness of God. We continue with the hope that students will reflect this love near and far. There is no greater example we can set.

REFLECTION QUESTIONS:

- How do I respond when asked why I chose this profession?

- When I think about religious diversity, what common themes come to mind?

- What is my definition of love?

- In what ways do, or can, I "will the good" of others?

- What kind of example will I be for students regarding religious diversity?

CONCLUSION

Hospitality, solidarity, and love are three beautiful concepts that can be made manifest in our everyday lives as student affairs practitioners. If we take great care to live our values, honor our faith and the faith of others, and channel God's love even in the most quotidian details of our work, we can improve the experience of the kaleidoscope of souls who enter our campuses every autumn in the hope of finding acceptance, understanding, and love.

Kristine Cyr Goodwin is vice president for student affairs at Providence College in Providence, Rhode Island.

REFERENCES

Ahmad, S. (February, 2016). "Living as a Muslim in a Catholic College." *America.* Retrieved from http://www.americamagazine.org/issue/interfaith-encounters.

Patel, E. (2007). *Acts of Faith.* Boston: Beacon Press.

Pope Francis. (2016). *For a Culture of Encounter.* Retrieved from https://w2.vatican.va/content/francesco/en/cotidie/2016/documents/papa-frances-co-cotidie_20160913_for-a-culture-of-encounter.html.

Hellwig, M. (1999). *Guests of God: Stewards of Divine Creation.* New York: Paulist Press.

CHAPTER 15

Race and Social Justice: Lessons from Ferguson and Saint Louis University

Mona Hicks and Kent Porterfield

In 2010, Adolfo Nicolas, SJ, 30th Superior General of the Society of Jesus, asked Jesuit colleges and universities, "What kind of encounter do we have with our students if we are not changed? And the meaning of change for our institutions is who our students become, what they value, and what they do later in life. To put it another way, a Jesuit education…[should] work toward constructing a more human, just, sustainable, and faith-filled world" (Nicolas, 2010). In 2014, between the late hours of Sunday, October 12 and the early hours of Monday, October 13, a "deep, real encounter" came to Saint Louis University (SLU) when nearly a thousand people protested at the university's Clock Tower. This protest, which became known as #OccupySLU, challenged the SLU community to affirm whether it could truly be a safe place for dialogue on the difficult social issues of racial inequality.

#OCCUPYSLU AND #FERGUSONOCTOBER

On August 9, 2014, unarmed African-American teenager Michael Brown was shot and killed by a white police officer, Darren Wilson, in Ferguson, Missouri. As context, SLU is located approximately 12 miles southeast of Ferguson. Almost immediately, African Americans in the Ferguson community reacted in grief and anger, demanding justice for the killing of Brown. On October 8, another African-American teenager, VonDerrit Myers, was shot and killed by an off-duty police officer. The Shaw neighborhood, where the killing took place, is located less than two miles from SLU's south campus, and Myers' father was a long-time SLU employee. Protests began almost immediately.

On Sunday, October 12, an interfaith prayer service titled "Hip, Hop, and Hope," was hosted in SLU's Chaifetz Arena and the complexities of racial inequality emerged. At around 1:30 a.m. on October 13, SLU's director of public safety contacted senior administrators to inform them that a group of more than a thousand protestors was marching toward SLU's main campus. Several SLU students were involved in the march. SLU's president agreed to allow the protestors to enter the campus. Earlier confrontations between protestors and law enforcement had resulted in intense confrontations and arrests, and SLU's president decided that a peaceful response was preferable to the use of authoritative force.

As protestors marched onto the campus, students came out of their residence halls, some joining in with the protestors, and others to see and experience what was happening. When the protestors arrived at SLU's Clock Tower, the march stopped and leaders spoke to the crowd. Over the next several hours, most of the protestors left campus, but about two dozen remained the following morning. They used social media to make requests for tents, food, water, and supplies. They intended to stay. Help came quickly, and #OccupySLU began.

Over the next five days, a communications center was established on campus to respond to telephone calls, e-mails, and social media, as well as mainstream media. A communications webpage was established and webcams were installed to allow concerned parties to observe what was happening in real time. Fueled by social media, #OccupySLU received national and international attention. While many applauded SLU for its peaceful response, others were harshly critical and demanded forcefully ousting the occupiers from campus (private property) and making arrests if necessary. SLU chose to resume normal campus operations to the fullest extent possible, to closely monitor activity at the Clock Tower, to increase public safety staffing, to promote campus dialogue through teach-ins and other programs, and to allow peaceful counter demonstrations and interactions at the Clock Tower. The occupiers were allowed to remain. As the week progressed, some benefactors threatened to pull their support, some parents demanded authoritative action, and a few students threatened to leave the university.

SLU did not remove the occupiers; rather, the university community listened and sought to understand. Faculty, students, staff, and administrators talked with protestors. Student affairs staff reached out to students to hear their concerns, engage them in dialogue, and provide support to help relieve their anxieties and tensions. Difficult topics of race, privilege, systemic oppression, and social justice were considered and addressed through a variety of campus programs.

By the end of the fifth day, after a series of meetings, a draft agreement was reached. The agreement, known as the Clock Tower Accords, outlined ways SLU would promote equity and educational success on campus and in St. Louis, as well as help promote economic development and opportunity in impoverished St. Louis neighborhoods. On Saturday, October 18, 2014, #OccupySLU ended.

LESSONS

As a result of #OccupySLU and #FergusonOctober, several issues and challenges were examined at SLU, including generational differences, social media, campus safety, social justice, and the roles student affairs educators can have as advocates and activists.

Generational differences. At SLU, generational differences were observed during #OccupySLU and #FergusonOctober. For example, older generations within the African-American community welcomed activists like Hedy Epstein, Dr. Cornel West, and NAACP President Cornell William Brooks as participants and speakers at the interfaith event. However, African-American youth involved in movements like Tribe X expressed frustration with these well-known and established activists, whom they criticized for accepting privileges and not making the progress needed to improve the quality of life for a new generation of African-American citizens. Additionally, while many of the parents were outspoken about campus safety concerns during #OccupySLU, most of the students did not express those same concerns, or not nearly to the same degree.

Social media. The new concept of the citizen journalist, combined with the effect that social media has on social behavior, was apparent during #OccupySLU. People tuned in constantly and reacted with "techno anxiety" to social media posts, e-mail and text messages, and tweets (Pew Research Center, 2010). It became impossible to track and respond to all the inquiries and media, and it was difficult to differentiate fact from fiction. In an age where digital technology is rapidly advancing, where students are fully engaged in social media, and where news coverage is non-stop, student affairs practice must adapt (Whitt et al., 2016).

Concepts of safety. Although students may not have understood all the complexities of #OccupySLU or the racial equality movement ignited by Michael Brown's death in Ferguson, relatively few expressed feeling unsafe. They did, however, acknowledge how uncomfortable it was to grapple with their societal privileges and advantages. One assumption made by some internal and external stakeholders was that #OccupySLU participants were not SLU students, which illustrated a clear bias about how they thought SLU students were supposed to look and act. In truth, the #OccupySLU protests *did* involve SLU students, and these students engaged other SLU students. Student interactions changed and evolved throughout the week of #OccupySLU, as did their sense of care, curiosity, and conviction. With dialogue, experience, and reflection, anecdotally many SLU students were better able to understand the difference between what it means to be "safe," and what it means to be "uncomfortable."

> "To work toward a goal of social justice, student affairs practice has to be about advocacy, not just awareness."

Complexities of teaching social justice. Teaching social justice across a diversity of races and developmental stages is a challenge. How does Catholic higher education mission intersect with the current socio-political aspects of race and social justice in the United States and abroad? As microaggressions are the most common form of racism perpetrated by students and others in a campus community, one practical suggestion might be to apply critical race theory in intentional ways to student affairs practice, as a means to expose and address the challenges, and move toward a more authentic dialogue and contemplative social action (Magolda & Baxter-Magolda, 2011).

Student affairs educators as advocates and activists. Catholic higher education institutions place a particular emphasis on working for and "on the side of the poor, marginalized, and those seeking justice" (Association of Jesuit Colleges and Universities, 2016, p. 15). To work toward a goal of social justice, student affairs practice has to be about advocacy, not just awareness (Magolda & Baxter-Magolda, 2011). #OccupySLU cast a brighter light on the importance of this point. Practically speaking, student affairs educators must sometimes disrupt the status quo with their everyday interactions to help dismantle systemic injustices and build more inclusive campus communities (Magolda & Baxter-Magolda, 2011).

SUMMARY

What did SLU students learn from #FergusonOctober and #OccupySLU? An argument can be made that what happened on campus during #OccupySLU produced an environment that was uncomfortable and unpredictable, but conducive to learning that might not otherwise have taken place. Such an environment is one that "help[s] students see that they are not only autonomous individuals, but also members of a larger community to which they are accountable" (Boyer, 1990, p. 54).

Thinking about the events that took place at SLU in October 2014, the words of Peter-Hans Kolvenbach, SJ, former superior general of the Society of Jesus, come to mind: "Students, in the course of their formation, must let the gritty reality of this world into their lives, so they can learn to feel, think about it critically, respond to its suffering and engage it constructively. They should learn to perceive, think, judge, choose, and act for the rights of others, especially the disadvantaged and the oppressed" (p. 8).

Mona Hicks is the associate vice president and dean of students and Kent Porterfield is the vice president for student development at Saint Louis University in St. Louis, Missouri.

REFERENCES

Association of Jesuit College and Universities. (2016). *Some Characteristics of Jesuit Colleges and Universities: A Self-evaluation Instrument.* Washington, DC: Author.

Boyer, E., & The Carnegie Foundation of the Advancement of Teaching. (1990). *Campus Life: In Search of Community.* Lawrenceville, NJ: Princeton University Press.

Kolvenbach, P.H. (2000). *The Service of Faith and the Promotion of Justice in American Jesuit Higher Education.* Address delivered at the Commitment to Justice in Jesuit Higher Education Conference, Santa Clara University, CA.

Magolda, P.M., & Baxter-Magolda, M.B. (2011). *Contested Issues in Student Affairs: Diverse Perspectives and Respectful Dialogue.* Sterling, VA: Stylus.

Nicolas, A. (2010). *Depth, Universality, and Learned Ministry: Challenges to Jesuit Higher Education Today.* Address delivered at the Conference for Jesuit Higher Education Institutions, Mexico City.

Pew Research Center. (2010). *Millennials: A Portrait of Generation Next.* Retrieved on July 9, 2015 from http://pewresearch.org/millenials.

Whitt, E.J., Roger, L.D., Porterfield, K.T., & Carnaghi, J.E. (2016). "Angst and Hope: Current Issues in Student Affairs Leadership." *New Directions for Student Services, 153.*

CHAPTER 16

Walking the Two-Way Bridge: Transgender at Catholic Colleges and Universities

Sandra M. Estanek

Lesbian, gay, bisexual, and transgender (LGBT) students attend Catholic institutions, and student affairs professionals are called to support their learning and development. This traditional role of student affairs regarding every one of their students is at the heart of Principle One and Catholic hospitality. Those who work at Catholic institutions find themselves at a complex and difficult intersection of professional obligations — to Church teaching, to professional standards, and to federal and state laws — as they work to serve their students. This chapter will suggest a context for how Catholic colleges and universities can strive to "welcome all students into a vibrant campus community that celebrates God's love for all" (Principle One).

PROFESSIONAL OBLIGATIONS: THE CATHOLIC CONTEXT

The starting point for a discussion of gender identity at Catholic colleges and universities is Catholic anthropology, that is, the Catholic understanding of the human person. Catholic theology is incarnational, which means that its starting point is that the person of Jesus is as fully human as He is fully God, "the Word made flesh" (Jn 1:14). Catholic incarnational theology understands that to be human is to be a "unity of body and soul" created "in the image and likeness of God" (*Catechism of the Catholic Church,* 2000, p. 93). Because each human person is created in the image and likeness of God, each person is possessed of an inherent and absolute dignity. This unity of body and soul is gendered: "male and female He created them" (Gn 1:26-28). The *Catechism of the Catholic Church* affirms two principles that undergird the Catholic understanding of gender identity: that binary (male or female) heterosexuality is normative and that every human person has inherent dignity and is equally deserving of respect.

First, the Church holds that binary heterosexuality is normative. "'Being man' or 'being woman' is a reality that is good and willed by God: Man and woman possess an inalienable dignity which comes to them immediately from God their Creator" (*Catechism of the Catholic Church,* 2000, p. 94). The purpose of this "complementarity of the sexes" is to transmit human life and thus to "cooperate in a unique way in the Creator's work" (*Catechism,* p. 95). Pope Francis in *Amoris Laetitia* (2016) reaffirmed this traditional understanding.

Second, while affirming the Catholic Church's understanding that binary heterosexuality is normative, the *Catechism* also affirms the dignity of all persons. The *Catechism* states that homosexual [sic] persons "must be accepted with respect, compassion, and sensitivity. Every sign of unjust discrimination in their regard should be avoided" (*Catechism of the Catholic Church,* 2000, p. 566).

PROFESSIONAL OBLIGATIONS: APA GUIDELINES

Fifty years of secular research has challenged this binary definition of gender as either male or female and has painted a different picture of gender as a continuum that includes same-sex sexual expression and, more recently understood, transgender. In 2015, the American Psychological Association (APA) published new guidelines for practice with transgender and gender non-conforming (TGNC) people. These guidelines inform student affairs professional standards and are utilized in student affairs practice. The APA affirms that, "[a] person's identification as TGNC can be healthy and self-affirming, and is not inherently pathological" (APA, 2015, p. 835). The guidelines state that TGNC people face societal stigma, discrimination, and microaggressions that may cause them to experience "distress associated with discordance between their gender identity and their body or sex assigned at birth" (APA, 2015, p. 835). The APA cites examples of discrimination in employment, housing, and health care, as well as social ostracizing, rejection by family, and even violence. Cited as microaggressions are refusal to acknowledge the person's gender identity, insensitive questions about one's body, and assuming that a TGNC person is "sick" and must be "cured" (APA, 2015).

The Catholic Church views this research with skepticism. Consistent with Catholic anthropology, Pope Francis wrote in *Amoris Laetitia* (2016), "Yet another challenge is posed by various forms of an ideology of gender that denies the difference and reciprocity in nature of a man and a woman... [C]onsequently, human identity becomes the choice of the individual, one which can also change over time" (pp. 44, 45). However, consistent with the inherent dignity of all human persons, Pope Francis also wrote: "[W]e also need to be humble and realistic, acknowledging that at times the way we present our Christian beliefs and treat other people has helped to contribute to today's problematic situation" (pp. 26-27).

PROFESSIONAL OBLIGATIONS: GOVERNMENT

In May 2016, the U.S. Departments of Justice and Education under the Obama administration issued a joint *Dear Colleague* letter that gave specific guidance for how institutions must support transgender students on campus to comply with their Title IX obligations. Many organizations, including the United States Conference of Catholic

Bishops, objected to this guidance as a violation of the First Amendment freedom of religion and an overreach by the federal government. The Trump administration rescinded that letter and its specific guidance in February 2017. However, the new *Dear Colleague* letter states that "withdrawal of these guidance documents does not leave students without protections from discrimination, bullying, or harassment. All schools must ensure that all students, including LGBT students, are able to learn and thrive in a safe environment" (U.S. Department of Education, 2017).

PRACTICAL APPLICATION: EMERGING IDEAS FOR DISCUSSION

The Catholic Church, the Department of Education, and the APA guidelines all decry discrimination against LGBT people but, in practice, do not share assumptions and do not agree on what to do. Student affairs professionals face the difficult challenge of translating what this means on a practical day-to-day level as they work with the LGBT community on Catholic campuses. This challenge is not unanticipated. Principle Two of the *Principles of Good Practice for Student Affairs at Catholic Colleges and Universities* states, "In addition to relevant civil law and professional standards of practice and ethics, scripture, tradition, philosophical reflection, and the sustained experience of the Christian community all help to guide policy formation and decision making in Catholic institutions." When questions arise, Principle Two suggests initiating discussions with mission officers, campus ministers, theology faculty, and Church and pastoral leaders as appropriate to assist student affairs professionals in developing a "way of proceeding" that is consistent with the expectation of this principle. This dialogue exists and now includes the topic of transgender.

Rev. James Martin, SJ, provides a possible resource for this dialogue in his October 30, 2016, article in *America* magazine, titled "A Two-Way Bridge." Martin begins with the recognition of the tensions between the LGBT community and the Catholic Church and asks how both sides can bridge this experience. He asks each to understand the other and treat the other with "respect, compassion, and sensitivity" called for by the *Catechism* (p. 1). He then calls for building a "two-way bridge" characterized by listening, understanding, and accompanying. Martin reminds those who work at Catholic colleges and universities that they only need to look to the example of Jesus himself for a path forward. "Jesus saw beyond categories; he met people where they were and accompanied them" (p. 6).

Catholic higher educational professional associations also have provided forums for participants to think through these issues together. The Association for Student Affairs at Catholic Colleges and Universities (ASACCU) held a one-day symposium following its 2016 annual conference titled *Called to Serve: Supporting Our LGBTQ*

> "The act of genuinely listening conveys the 'respect, compassion, and sensitivity' that the Catholic Church calls for in the Catechism."

Students at Catholic Institutions. The theme of the 2017 annual meeting of the Association of Catholic Colleges and Universities (ACCU) was *Inclusion on Campus: Exploring Diversity as an Expression of God's Grandeur* and included a session on "Serving the LGBTQ Community" from a Catholic perspective. A pre-conference for student affairs professionals held prior to the 2017 ACCU meeting also included a session on "Faithful Catholic Hospitality to LGBT Students." The ideas that emerged in these discussions echo themes found in Martin's article: listening, understanding, and accompanying. For student affairs professionals on campus "listening, understanding, and accompanying" have practical day-to-day applications and raise difficult questions. What follows are ideas from some institutions that may assist Catholic colleges and universities in their own "bridge building" discussions on campus.

One of the ideas that was most generally accepted by those at the meetings cited above, consistent with Martin's article, was that student affairs professionals need to listen to transgender students on campus and ask them what they are experiencing, and what they need, instead of presuming to know. The act of genuinely listening conveys the "respect, compassion, and sensitivity" that the Catholic Church calls for in the *Catechism*. While immediately referring transgender students to counseling could be considered a microaggression, the counseling office, health center, diversity office, and campus ministry can be powerful allies, if they are prepared to do so. Providing in-service education for professional staff will help them frame and process what they hear from transgender students in the context of the institution's Catholic identity and university mission.

Some Catholic institutions already have gay and lesbian "allies" groups that can provide a vehicle of communication and bridge building. These peer groups can be supportive communities for transgender students; however, they may need guidance to appropriately include the different experiences and needs of transgender students. They may also need guidance in understanding Catholic teaching to help craft a path forward.

Attendees at the various forums also posed practical day-to-day questions, raising issues that point to the need for institutions to initiate discussions on campus in advance of requests from individual students. Doing so will help staff know what to do and students know that their requests were anticipated. Four examples were advanced:

1. The importance of being addressed by our preferred name is something we all desire. It is a powerful act of respect and recognition. Extending this respect to others can take the form of addressing all students, including transgender students, with each student's preferred name in class, in the registrar's office, or on stage at commencement.

2. Filling out forms with ease is something we all desire. Having staff review paperwork and streamline forms — from admissions through alumni records — by removing unnecessary gender references assists everyone.

3. All students desire to live in a safe and supportive environment while on campus, especially in residence halls. One way to communicate that is to ask, "Would you prefer a single room?" Supportive roommates may be identified by asking, "Would you be an affirming roommate for a transgender person? Yes? No? Unsure?" Queries such as these give students options and reveal a college's desire to provide a positive atmosphere for all.

4. Many people are uncomfortable being unclothed around others regardless of gender expression. One path forward is to frame the issue of bathroom usage as one of privacy rather than gender. Institutions can affirm this by placing locks on doors of public single-seat restrooms and replacing the "men" and "women" designations with signs simply reading "restroom." In large multi-person bathrooms, placing shower curtains on the dressing area outside each shower assists and acknowledges individual privacy.

The experience of transgender students challenges all higher education professionals to ask new questions and accompany students in new ways, only some of which have been mentioned here. Student affairs professionals at Catholic colleges and universities have an opportunity to facilitate, and even lead, these discussions on campus. A popular fad a few years ago was to wear wristbands that said WWJD ("What would Jesus do?"). This question could be a good place for student affairs professionals at Catholic colleges and universities to begin.

Sandra M. Estanek is a professor of graduate education and leadership and director of the higher education and student affairs administration master's program at Canisius College in Buffalo, New York.

REFERENCES

American Psychological Association. (2015). Guidelines of Psychological Practice with Transgender and Gender Non-conforming People. *American Psychologist,* 70(9), 832-864. doi: 10.1037/a0039906.

Catholic Church. (2000). *Catechism of the Catholic Church* [English translation] (2nd ed.). Vatican City: Liberia Editrice Vaticana.

Martin, J. (2016, October 30). "A Two-Way Bridge." *America.* Retrieved from http://www.americamagazine.org/issue/two-way-bridge.

Pope Francis. (2016). *Amoris laetitia.* Retrieved from http://w2.vatican.va/content/dam/francesco/pdf/apost_exhortations/documents/papa-francesco_esortazi-one-ap_20160319_amoris-laetitia_en.pdf.

U.S. Department of Education & U.S. Department of Justice. (2017, February). *Dear Colleague.* Retrieved from https://findit.ed.gov/search?utf8=%E2%9C%93&affili-ate=ed.gov&query=dear+colleague+higher+education+2017+transgender&com-mit=Search.

PRINCIPLE TWO

Grounds policies, practices, and decisions in the teachings and living tradition of the Church. Builds and prepares the student affairs staff to make informed contributions to the Catholic mission of the institution.

CHAPTER 17 Developing a Catholic Culture: Catholic Cultural Competency as a Critical Skill **103**

Josh A. Hengemuhle, University of St. Thomas (MN)

CHAPTER 18 Making Mission Matter: Recruitment and Supervision of Mission **109**

John Felio and Jabrina Robinson, Siena College

CHAPTER 19 Onboarding for Mission **113**

Jennifer Mussi Nolan, Fordham University

CHAPTER 20 Assessing the Impact of Student Affairs on Mission **117**

Erin R. Ebersole, Immaculata University

CHAPTER 17

Developing a Catholic Culture: Catholic Cultural Competency as a Critical Skill

Josh A. Hengemuhle

Morey and Piderit (2006) wrote of a culture in crisis, arguing that Catholic higher education was at risk of losing its distinctiveness. In their analysis, Catholic colleges and universities were beginning to look increasingly like other institution of higher education. Crisis or not, many student affairs professionals throughout Catholic higher education recognize that the culture has shifted in recent decades. Given that more of us working within student affairs at Catholic colleges and universities do not have formal training related to Catholic culture and identity (Schaller & Boyle, 2006), engaging Catholic culture within our work is no longer second nature. If student affairs leadership at Catholic colleges and universities wants to maintain the claim of distinctiveness — that there is something unique about the way we do our work because of being a Catholic institution — it is critical they take steps to actively inform the cultural understanding within their divisions.

An initial shift to be made is to implement Catholic cultural understanding as a necessary *competency* to be assessed and developed. Working at a Catholic institution is distinctive within higher education, and professionals who can demonstrate competency in knowing how the Catholic culture influences their work better serve the institution. This is not to say individuals practicing within Catholic colleges or universities must be Catholic; rather, a broad and foundational understanding of Catholic culture is important to their work. Comparatively, working within other distinctive institutions, like historically Black colleges or universities (HBCUs), women's colleges, Hispanic-Serving Institutions (HSIs), or tribal colleges, it is not essential, nor should it be, for an individual working within any of these institutions to claim the corresponding identity. However, it is essential for them to possess, or at minimum be actively developing, an understanding of that identity, its history, and its cultural significance.

Many of us within Catholic higher education are familiar with the idea of "hiring for mission" (Estanek, Herdlein, & Harris, 2011) as common language for how our institution's Catholic identity affects our hiring decisions. Bringing the understanding of Catholic cultural competency into the search and hiring process requires an assessment of a candidate's competency. Supervisors might consider asking questions such as, "How do you see Catholic identity influencing the work you would do here?" "What familiarity do you have with *Ex corde Ecclesiae* or other documents related to Catholic higher education?" or "Tell us about your experience related to our order's charism." These questions engage the applicant in rich discussion and signal to the incoming staff that Catholic cultural competency is a central tenet of the work at the institution. These are not questions aimed at discerning the candidate's own religious identity but rather to assess their understanding of — or willingness to engage with — the culture in which they will be working, if hired.

An interview process makes explicit the Catholic identity of the institution and the idea that that identity is an integral part of the work, and it is only the beginning of developing an intentional Catholic culture in student affairs. If cultural identity is not frequently explored and engaged by each staff member beyond the hiring process, it will not come to fruition. A fuller integration of the Catholic culture into one's ways of operating requires robust socialization (Chatman, 1991). Socialization is the process by which an individual encounters, and takes on as their own, the norms, customs, and values of a culture (Schein, 2010). Socialization is not a one-time effort but rather must occur with repetition to maintain and strengthen cultural norms. Examining socialization within our divisions allows us to expand the focus beyond hiring for mission to include methods used to develop the employee's competency to work within the existing culture, and an employee's capacity for that development. Leveraging socialization to shape a culture that is in alignment with our institution's particular charism or expression of Catholic identity is extremely important.

One critical way to direct socialization is through regular formal trainings, including department or division retreats, speaker series, monthly or quarterly workshops, reading groups, and other similar opportunities. In fact, a study of senior student affairs professionals at Catholic colleges and universities revealed many senior-level student affairs officers working at Catholic colleges and universities considered newly hired student affairs professionals to be unprepared to work within the context of a Catholic institution (Schaller & Boyle, 2006; Estanek, Herdlein, & Harris, 2011). Any training or development of this cultural understanding within new staff becomes the responsibility of those already working within the institution and supervising those professionals. Typically, student affairs professionals accomplish this through either supporting external professional development opportunities or developing and promoting internal trainings (Estanek et al., 2011).

Training sessions on Catholic identity represent formal efforts toward cultural socialization (Morgan, 2006), and most student affairs professionals participate in formal training related to student affairs practice (Estanek, 2002). Heeding Estanek's call for student affairs practitioners at Catholic colleges and universities to be transcultural (Estanek, 2002), formal training in the Catholic culture of the institution is critical. The institution can execute this training or elect to send staff members to external trainings. Viewing Catholic cultural understanding as a necessary competency for practice requires investing resources into ensuring the staff develops this competency.

However, active formation of a culture focused on implementing the Catholic identity of the institution should be even more pervasive. Culture is dynamic, not static. Everyone in the organization creates culture by what they think,

> "Everyone in the organization creates culture by what they think, say, and do."

say, and do. Culture is led from the top down, but it comes to life from the bottom up (Gordon, 2010). Creating structures and patterns to encourage this "bottom-up" life to develop is the task of student affairs leadership. Accomplishing this requires expanding the idea of Catholic cultural competency beyond the occasional training session or hiring process and into the day-in, day-out operations of the division. For this transition to occur, it is imperative each student affairs staff member sees implementation of Catholic cultural identity as part of her or his individual responsibilities. Too often student affairs staff seeking to engage the Catholic nature of the institution turn to colleagues in campus ministry or related departments to bear the load. Student affairs collaboration and consultation with campus ministry is important, but not if we abdicate our own responsibility in fostering Catholic identity on campus.

A comparison may again be in order. Multicultural competency and an ability to serve diverse students are increasingly expected of every student affairs practitioner (ACPA, 1997). Few student affairs professionals who are well-versed in the current discussions in the field would wholly defer responsibility for advancing multiculturalism and inclusion to the "diversity office" on campus. Multicultural competence is incorporated broadly into our work within student affairs. A similar understanding within Catholic higher education must take shape around Catholic identity, rather than it becoming or remaining only the purview of campus ministry offices. In fact, this is the level of engagement that the *Principles of Good Practice* call us to act upon.

A concrete way to ensure more staff accept responsibility for engaging the Catholic identity of the institution is to incorporate it into formal and informal evaluation. Practitioners can begin by reflecting on how often the Catholic identity of the institution and its influence on their work comes up in regular supervisory conversations. Often, if the topic comes up at all, it occurs when there are barriers or difficulties continuing to challenge the understanding of Catholic identity as a positive influence on our work (Estanek, 2002). Perhaps if it was a regular topic broached by the supervisor, staff would develop an understanding of it as important and actively seek ways in which to demonstrate to their supervisor their engagement with the topic. Similarly, if questions of engaging Catholic culture were included in formal employee evaluations, student affairs staff would come to understand these performance criteria as important aspects of the institution and their work.

For much of the history of Catholic higher education, our institutions were led and operated by individuals deeply formed in the culture of the Catholic Church. Because of this, the Catholic culture was naturally woven into the fabric of the institution. With greater lay leadership, shifting cultural understandings outside the Church, and a nation more pluralistic than ever before, the Catholic culture of our institutions may become slowly diluted over time, slipping from our focus. Understanding the nature of culture within an organization, as well as how Catholic cultural competency can influence it, equips us to take concrete action toward the development of a renewed understanding of what we want the culture to be and to actively work to influence it. Morey and Piderit (2006) tell us we can no longer take the Catholic cultural foundation of our institutions for granted. Rather, it falls to us, the new leaders in Catholic higher education, to ensure we guard that tradition and work toward its realization in our work.

Josh A. Hengemuhle is an assistant dean of students at the University of St. Thomas in St. Paul, Minnesota.

REFERENCES

American College Personnel Association. (1997). *Principles of Good Practice for Student Affairs.*

Chatman, J. A. (1991). "Matching People and Organizations: Selection and Socialization in Public Accounting Firms." *Administrative Science Quarterly* 36, 459-484.

Estanek, S. M., Herdlein, R. & Harris, J. (2011). "Preparation of New Professionals and Mission-Driven Hiring Practices: A Survey of Senior Student Affairs Officers at Catholic Colleges and Universities." *College Student Affairs Journal* 29(2), 151-163.

Gordon, J. (2010). *Soup: A Recipe to Create a Culture of Greatness.* Hoboken, NJ: John Wiley & Sons Inc.

Morey, M. M. & Piderit, J. J. (2006). *Catholic Higher Education: A Culture in Crisis.* New York: Oxford University Press.

Schaller, M. A. & Boyle, K. M. (2006). "Student Affairs Professionals at Catholic Colleges and Universities: Honoring Two Philosophies." *Catholic Education: A Journal of Inquiry and Practice* 10(2), 163-180.

Schein, E. H. (2010). *Organizational Culture and Leadership* (4th ed.). San Francisco: Jossey-Bass.

CHAPTER 18

Making Mission Matter: Recruitment and Supervision of Mission

John Felio and Jabrina Robinson

Recently, while listening to a National Public Radio broadcast, the host referenced John F. Kennedy's first visit to NASA headquarters, which occurred in 1961. The host explained that while touring the facility, the president introduced himself to a janitor and asked what he did at NASA. The janitor replied, "I'm helping put a man on the moon!" While there is no evidence that this interaction actually took place, it is a great anecdote for this chapter.

How do we supervise and evaluate for mission in Catholic higher education? Does our staff, like the NASA janitor, connect their specific job responsibilities to the much larger mission and, if so, how? As student affairs practitioners, we decided to explore this topic through the lens of our own campus, beginning with a similar question to a student affairs staff member at Siena College. "How do you incorporate mission into your work?" That person responded: "As I approach my eleventh year at Siena, my role in student life has helped me better understand that the Franciscan mission is integral and vital to my job and daily life. As an advisor and mentor to club leaders, orientation leaders, student senate, class councils, and student employees, teaching them to understand and reflect upon mission is the most challenging and rewarding part of my responsibilities."

RECRUITMENT FOR MISSION

To effectively supervise and assess for mission, it is imperative that we are attentive to our recruitment of new student affairs staff from the initial employment posting through the interview process. Does your job posting state that candidates should articulate, in their cover letter, how they can contribute to the mission of your institution? As a hiring supervisor, this certainly helps narrow the candidate pool. Some candidates neglect to reference mission in their cover letter, which may be a "cut and paste" form letter. Other candidates use this opportunity to share their specific interest in your institution's mission. For example, in a recent job search an applicant wrote the following in their cover letter: "My view of community and student life, framed in the Franciscan and Catholic traditions, is based on faith and

> "Successful candidates engage interviewers with enthusiasm and thoughtful questions about mission."

service. It is an inspired and actively engaged student body that works collaboratively to address social injustices." This explicit reference to mission serves as a model to distinguish promising candidates.

Once you identify candidates to interview on campus, what information relating to mission do you provide them in preparation for their interview? Examples of materials we send to candidates include copies of Siena College's *DORS Initiative* brochure, which outlines our Catholic and Franciscan values and how we use these values to frame our work in the division; and *The Seven Tenets of Franciscan Education*. We do not expect candidates to become "experts" on Catholic Social Teaching or our Franciscan mission. However, we do incorporate questions into our interview process that seek to elicit a candidate's commitment to mission, understanding of uniqueness of working at a religiously affiliated institution, and excitement of learning more about mission. Unsuccessful candidates tend to respond to questions about mission from memorized portions of these materials. Successful candidates engage interviewers with enthusiasm and thoughtful questions about mission.

Once you have made your hiring decision, how does your commitment to recruit for mission transition to supervision and evaluation practices?

INTEGRATION OF MISSION

As student affairs professionals, we have a responsibility to create a mission-centered culture. In the midst of our daily tasks, we must avoid losing sight of mission. There is greater clarity in day-to-day decision making when priorities and goals are aligned with mission. To ensure thorough integration, mission planning should be included in everything from student activities programming to the designing of the residential housing selection process. Student affairs leadership is responsible for anchoring our division's work to mission and to ensure the integration, mindful reflection, and evaluation of that goal.

Over the years, our student affairs division has driven several mission-integrated initiatives to provide more tangible articulation of Siena's Franciscan and Catholic values. The goal is to translate mission into concrete specifics that are easily understood by staff and students. In fall 2015, Vice President for Student Life Maryellen Gilroy and Professor of Religious Studies and Friar in Residence Rev. Dennis Tamburello, OFM, worked together to develop *Habits of Franciscan Community*. These *Habits* provide a shared understanding of celebrating each person's God-given uniqueness as we welcome and support one another in an inclusive community. The eight practices of the *Habits of Franciscan Community* are brotherhood/sisterhood, faith, prayer, hospitality, inclusion of the other, respect, common good, and peace.

In our annual student affairs division retreat, the *Habits of Franciscan Community* were shared and discussed. Our professional staff quickly adapted and incorporated these habits into residence assistant training to reinforce the way student leaders live out the mission. Throughout the year, the residence assistants further shared these habits with their students through programming. A Twitter campaign led by residential life staff, titled #cultivatethehabit, provided inspirational quotes and relevant messaging around the *Habits of Franciscan Community*.

By making Siena's mission more easily understood, the *Habits of Franciscan Community* provided a new and engaging approach to sharing mission that began with student affairs senior leadership and was, ultimately, embraced by students. As one student leader said, "The Habits allow us to really create a community where everyone feels safe and part of the community. The habits all go together to help create this community where everyone is included."

ASSESSMENT AND SUPERVISION OF MISSION

Assessing for mission provides an avenue to evaluate how each department has demonstrated a commitment to the college mission through educational outreach, programs, and services. Acknowledging and rewarding successful mission-centered achievements helps engrain the importance of our college's identity into the student experience. The assessment process provides time and space for us to reflect and discuss the ways we can hold our departments, and our division as a whole, accountable for achieving the mission of the college.

Departments within student affairs are asked to approach the assessment process as an important tool to inform our work and improve operations. Each year, our vice president provides divisional themes related to our college mission that must be assessed as part of each department's student learning outcomes. For the 2015–2016 academic year, one theme asked, How has your department demonstrated a commitment to the Siena College mission through educational outreach, services, or operationally? Eight student affairs departments led 15 quantitative and qualitative assessments to measure this commitment. Sample projects included:

- The Office of Compliance incorporating mission and values discussions during the Clery Act compliance training; and

- The Damietta Cross-Cultural Center drawing direct connections between mission and being an ally to LGBTQ students during ally training for students, faculty, and staff.

The review of these mission-focused assessments highlighted paths to continue collaboration in promoting mission and purposeful outreach. Additional examples of how supervision for mission is incorporated into our department include annual mission-focused retreats for student affairs professional staff; mission-related student learning outcomes for all departments as part of our assessment efforts; routine discussions at all levels of staff meetings (including student staff) that are mission-based (articles, inviting guest speakers, policies, programs, etc.); opening meetings with a prayer; and prioritizing professional development opportunities that are mission-focused.

CONCLUSION

Student affairs professionals can create value by aligning the mission of the college with their divisional strategies, culture, and performance measures. Mission-driven leadership is required, at all levels, to engage staff to find and achieve purpose in their work. Many student affairs professionals come to our campuses with varied understandings of Catholic traditions. Mission provides a common framework for the various roles throughout student affairs. Student affairs leaders must develop a common language of purpose and vision when articulating the college's mission. We should be able to articulate to students how any college program, from orientation through senior week, is distinct as it relates to our mission and to that of Catholic higher education.

This understanding of mission and Catholic higher education provides the foundation for co-curricular learning opportunities and compels student affairs practitioners to weave Catholic traditions and teachings into our work in service of students. As we strive to achieve this integration, we must hold our departments and divisions accountable to continuously review our purposeful delivery of mission.

John Felio is associate vice president for student life and Jabrina Robinson is dean of students at Siena College in Loudonville, New York.

CHAPTER 19

Onboarding for Mission

Jennifer Mussi Nolan

Onboarding for mission is critical to the practice of student affairs in Catholic higher education, given the dramatic decrease of members of sponsoring religious organizations who assume leadership and administrative roles on the campuses of American Catholic colleges and universities. Recent studies continue to illuminate the need for an ongoing effort to orient new staff to institutional mission and make staff training and development in mission a priority. Research recommendations help outline practical strategies for administrators to utilize when considering mission orientation and professional development opportunities.

WHAT WE'VE LEARNED ABOUT ONBOARDING FOR MISSION

A study titled, "Does Mission Matter?" examined the relationship between mission and new student affairs professionals at Jesuit institutions of American higher education. No single, consistent model of mission orientation was present at any of the campuses studied. While most new professionals interviewed said mission mattered to them, many lacked a foundational knowledge of Jesuit and Catholic mission. Furthermore, new professionals voiced concern regarding their confidence in engaging students in mission and did not evaluate their own knowledge of mission favorably. Because much of the work entrusted to new student affairs professionals involves engaging our students on the front lines, as a community we need to work harder to develop confidence in mission (Mussi, 2008).

A 2011 survey of mission-driven hiring practices and senior student affairs officers (SSAOs) at Catholic colleges and universities discovered that SSAOs "do not consider new professionals to be very well-prepared to work at Catholic colleges and universities" (Estanek, Herdlein, & Harris, 2011). The study confirms that much of the on-the-job training related to Catholic mission rests with the institution itself and Catholic professional development associations.

As a community of Catholic higher education educators and administrators, we need to vigorously approach the challenge of onboarding new staff for mission. We must create an environment in which we effectively onboard new staff for mission and foster career-long learning in mission. There are three distinct categories in

> "Supervisors must encourage and reward mission-centered professional development."

which we may focus and organize the efforts: (1) new staff orientation; (2) recurring professional development opportunities; and (3) ongoing staff supervision. A fourth category encompasses these three and serves as a general goal for the effort: having the courage to be creative and engaging when it comes to how we approach mission education.

NEW STAFF ORIENTATION

In the research examining orientation programs, one model emerged that addressed mission from an institutional, student affairs, and departmental perspective. This three-tiered approach emerged as a best-practice model for other Catholic institutions. New employees from across the institution were brought together by human resources to discuss a variety of new hire topics; also included was designated time to learn more about the sponsoring religious organization's tradition and the Catholic mission of their place of employment. This is an opportunity in which mission officers or members of the sponsoring religions communities can be of assistance. Similarly, the student affairs departments brought together their new hires to discuss mission through the lens of student affairs work and provided time for staff to participate in a mission-centric presentation. Finally, individual departments offered new staff training grounded in mission and focused on how the mission transcends their work in residence halls, student activities, counseling, and the like. For institutions considering such a model, topics covered in mission orientation workshops may include histories of the religious order, histories of the institution, and campus walking tours noting the various symbols, buildings, artifacts, and statuary on the campus.

PROFESSIONAL DEVELOPMENT OPPORTUNITIES AND BECOMING CAREER-LONG LEARNERS OF MISSION

Fostering an environment in which we can both build staff confidence and develop their competencies in mission was another area for improvement identified. Institutions should set aside resources (both time and money) for professional development related to mission. Supervisors must encourage and reward mission-centered professional development. The daily work of student affairs will always be present, but the staff retreat, Catholic-focused book club meeting, or mission-related guest speaker might be available only on occasion during the academic year. Helping staff and supervisors prioritize responsibilities and make time for participation in these programs is a way to create a culture of career-long learning about mission. Supervisors must serve as role models for this career-long approach to learning. Encouraging staff presence at liturgies, programs, and events is essential and staff should be encouraged and acknowledged for participating in these programs.

If programs that assist in this important work are not readily available or accessible on campus, there should be an institutional effort to create or advocate for them. Networking with other Catholic colleges and universities, local parishes and dioceses, and professional development organizations to participate in lectures or other mission-related programming that might not be available or practical to create on campus is one approach. Making a concerted effort to discover best practices in ongoing mission-centric professional development is another opportunity.

MISSION AND ONGOING SUPERVISION

Perhaps an efficient way to approach career-long learning about mission is through regular conversations at the departmental level between supervisors and staff. The staff's understanding of mission should be regularly discussed, rather than limited to the response to the "crisis du jour." Often, we are too busy muddling through an endless to-do list to stop and talk about ways in which we've seen intersections between mission and practice. Yet, these conversations are the ones that most resonate with new staff and our students.

Before we can expect departmental supervisors to be the stewards of onboarding new staff for mission and serving as the primary staff member who revisits mission education on a regular basis, we must train the trainers. A study titled *Exploring the Supervision Experiences of Student Affairs Mid-level Leaders in Catholic Higher Education* (Wenzel, 2013) asked mid-level supervisors to self-evaluate their efforts to train staff in mission. The supervisors reported they could be doing more and said they learned their supervision and training skills in mission through on-the-job experience and by watching past or current supervisors.

When considering this supervision study alongside the study of new professionals, it may indicate that we need to help supervisors get comfortable with the often uncomfortable conversation surrounding mission. Here is where seasoned SSAOs and departmental supervisors can lend their experience to establish a true teaching and learning environment among staff. Supervisors need to invite new staff members to observe and participate in those oftentimes complex conversations about policies and programming that may contradict aspects of our Catholic identity. Supervisors might ask staff members for their thoughts on a public controversy at another Catholic college or university reported by the media. Supervisors need to take time to proactively talk about how mission is alive in our daily work, not just during times when we find ourselves reacting to hot-button topics that put our mission and our work in a negative context. If we get comfortable with the discomfort that we often feel during challenging mission moments, we may find more of those moments are teachable for staff.

HAVING THE COURAGE TO BE CREATIVE

Finally, we must approach mission education with the courage to be creative. How can we challenge ourselves to be engaging in topics related to mission and find ways to be creative in our mission programming? We need to take advantage of technology to deliver mission facts and reminders on an ongoing basis. We need to partner with the veteran campus historian who seemingly knows everything about the sponsoring religious order. We need to meet with the priests, nuns, and brothers and conduct our own campus oral history projects. When we get out of our functional silos and collaborate across the university, great things can happen. Onboarding for mission is a perfect home for these types of creative collaborations, if we take the time and have the courage to make it happen.

Jennifer Mussi Nolan is an adjunct faculty member and former administrator at Fordham University in New York City, New York.

REFERENCES

Estanek, S. M., Herdlein, R., & Harris, J. (2011). Preparation of New Professional and Mission-Driven Hiring Practices: A Survey of Senior Student Affairs Officers at Catholic Colleges and Universities. *College Student Affairs Journal*, 29(2), 151-163.

Mussi, J. M. (2008). *Does Mission Matter? Exploring the Relationship Between the Mission of Jesuit Higher Education and New Student Affairs Professionals* (doctoral dissertation). Retrieved from ETD Collection for Fordham University. Paper AAI3312058.

Wenzel, D. A. (2013). *Exploring the Supervision Experiences of Student Affairs Mid-level Leaders in Catholic Higher Education* (doctoral dissertation). Retrieved from ETD Collection for Fordham University. Paper AAI3561733.

CHAPTER 20

Assessing the Impact of Student Affairs on Mission

Erin R. Ebersole

INTRODUCTION

In today's competitive market, colleges and universities must proactively provide evidence that they are delivering on the educational promises specified in their mission. While these promises may vary for each institution, Catholic colleges and universities are faced with the task of justifying the additional variables associated with an institutional mission focused on the holistic development of students' faith, values, and service. Student affairs practitioners often play a pivotal role in providing the holistic aspects of an educational experience. The following questions require us to consider how the work of student affairs can affect higher education:

1. What effect does student affairs have on students regarding the value-added components of the Catholic mission of the institution?

2. How can we assess the effect of student affairs on the holistic experience of the institutional mission?

3. Does being a Catholic institution make a difference in the educational outcomes of an institution and if so, how does the work of student affairs strengthen this effect?

4. This chapter provides practical suggestions for tackling these questions.

THEORETICAL PERSPECTIVE

With the evolution of effective learning modalities, the traditional classroom is being used less often and the opportunity for deep and meaningful student learning, which happens out of the classroom, needs to be effectively assessed by student affairs practitioners. For example, "deep learning" can happen during service trips, while living in residence halls, and during athletic competitions. These are just a few opportunities for co-curricular learning. Student affairs practitioners are critical to the success of the student educational experience and to ensuring that Catholic colleges and universities are upholding the promises made in their mission.

REFLECTIVE PERSPECTIVE

In 15 years of assessment work at Catholic institutions, I have seen firsthand how critical the co-curricular experience is to providing students with a holistic education. I have witnessed how student affairs programmatic efforts can surpass academic affairs in effective learning because of the personal development of competencies and skills that will assist a student for a lifetime. However, it has been my experience that, critical to the success of the good work student affairs does is the collaborative effort between student affairs and academic affairs. This can be accomplished by providing an "educational net" that ensures both areas provide learning opportunities for students to gain theoretical knowledge, as well as practical skills, through a shared set of student learning outcomes to which the entire institution is committed and leadership supports.

PRACTICAL PERSPECTIVE

The work of student affairs plays a critical role in ensuring that the mission of Catholic colleges and universities is realized in our students and can be articulated by our graduates. Catholic institutions need to be proactive in addressing current issues and challenges facing the world. They must assist students in their personal development as they prepare to enter the global society in which they will address issues of diversity (gender, ethnicity, sexuality, etc.) and technology (communication, information availability, social media, etc.). It is incumbent on Catholic institutions of higher education to assess a multitude of learning opportunities for students, as part of the educational experience, in a thoughtful and strategic way that is conducive to individual learning styles.

We know that the number of students attending Mass or going into vocations is not a valid measurement of the effectiveness of Catholic colleges and universities. Although there are data to support the effect that service trips have on students' holistic development, simply counting these experiences does not determine the outcome. As the number of students who self-identity as Catholic and attend Catholic institutions decreases, additional measures to assess the comprehensive value of Catholic higher education are needed, and student affairs plays a critical role in articulating this learning.

ASSESSING IMPACT

There are numerous ways in which student affairs practitioners can assess the impact their division has on students at Catholic colleges and universities. A few examples, described below, are meant to foster thought about different ways to perform assessments that show the effectiveness of Catholic higher education.

Assessment of the Institutional Mission Statement

One of the simplest ways to assess the impact of an institution's mission is to break down the mission statement and assess the contribution and influence of student affairs on the mission. Though an indirect assessment measure, this can show evidence to support the impact. For example, at a small Jesuit institution located in California, the mission statement reads:

> *The University pursues its vision by creating an academic community that educates the whole person within the Jesuit, Catholic tradition, making student learning our central focus, continuously improving our curriculum and co-curriculum, strengthening our scholarship and creative work, and serving the communities of which we are a part in Silicon Valley and around the world.*

To show evidence of the impact of this mission statement, one could gather data from students by asking them, "To what degree has your educational experience at this college impacted your development as a whole person?" To follow up, one could collect data from members of the Silicon Valley community and measure their view of the effect the college has had on their students' whole person development.

Assessment of Student Affairs Student Learning Outcomes

Having specific Student Affairs Student Learning Outcomes (SASLOs) within a division of student affairs is necessary for assessing the impact of the co-curricular experience on learning. In doing so, having clear SASLOs provides an opportunity for all members of the campus (students, faculty, and staff) to understand the importance of their work in an evidenced-based way. For example, at a small Catholic institution in Pennsylvania, the division of student affairs created a set of SASLOs that are clearly communicated and embedded in all co-curricular activities. One outcome states, "Students will learn and develop effective leadership skills as evidenced by: Demonstrating effective decision making and problem solving."

Assessment Using the "Principles of Good Practice for Student Affairs at Catholic Colleges and Universities"

The eight principles highlighted in this book can be used to guide colleges and universities through a qualitative assessment of holistic outcomes, which can cultivate a rich assessment process. Each of the eight principles is followed by five probing questions that will lead the student affairs practitioner to explore the effectiveness by developing an SLO to support such. For example, for Principle Five: "Challenges students to high standards of personal behavior and responsibility through the formation of character and virtues," Question 2c asks, "How do student affairs staff members help students develop the capacity for responsible decision making that is informed by Church teaching?" An institution could use this format to frame learning that has occurred in the students' personal development. Specifically, an institution could collect qualitative narrative about specific learning experiences that have shaped a student's character and virtues.

By considering these practical guidelines to assess the impact of student affairs work on student development and the mission of Catholic institutions of higher education, student affairs practitioners may be better equipped to address questions of educational value and accountability.

Erin R. Ebersole is the director of institutional research, planning, and effectiveness at Immaculata University in Malvern, Pennsylvania.

PRINCIPLE THREE

Enriches student integration of faith and reason through provision of co-curricular learning opportunities.

CHAPTER 21 Genuine Collaboration Between Student   123
Affairs and Academic Affairs

*Terri L. Mangione and Margaret Cain
McCarthy, Canisius College*

CHAPTER 22 The Changing Role of the Athletic Director   129

Jay DeFruscio, Atlantic 10 Conference

CHAPTER 23 Working with Controversial Speakers and   133
Events on a Catholic Campus

Todd A. Olson, Georgetown University

CHAPTER 21

Genuine Collaboration Between Student Affairs and Academic Affairs

Terri L. Mangione and Margaret Cain McCarthy

This chapter introduces an authentic, distinctive collaboration between student affairs (SA) and academic affairs (AA) in Catholic higher education, differentiated from basic campus partnerships. We share a concrete example, followed by what we have learned, as we work to institutionalize this distinct relationship on our Jesuit campus at Canisius College. This effort is a work in progress and requires constant commitment and determination to maintain a sustainable, collaborative effort between SA and AA. Within Catholic higher education, the value of community and the tradition of fostering the development of the whole person positions SA and AA to effectively apply an integrated approach to fostering a seamless learning experience for our students.

CONSIDER THE CONTEXT

In spring 2013, faced with a declining undergraduate population and first-to-second-year retention rate, along with a trustee-funded institutional analysis from an external consultant, the president of Canisius College commissioned a Retention Task Force. Senior leadership strongly believed that for a Retention Task Force to be successful, both SA and AA needed to be heavily invested. The authors, then the dean of students and the associate vice president for academic affairs, were appointed by the president as co-chairs of the task force.

The task force included key administrators from SA and AA, as well as many faculty members, 50 members in total. The president charged the task force to conduct a comprehensive study into the college's performance on retention and graduation rates to determine the root causes of the problem and develop a plan for improvement. Through weekly meetings, task force members painstakingly reviewed data, listened to one another's ideas, discussed, wrote, addressed the president's charges, and submitted our report. The final recommendations were comprehensive and inclusive. All were accepted and acted upon, including creation of the Griff Center for Academic Engagement, which reports jointly to the vice presidents for SA and AA. The Griff Center realigned the organizational structure to integrate services (freshman and transfer advisement, accessibility support, career services, veterans support, new student orientation, and tutoring) that are functionally related from the perspective of the student, eliminating silos and creating a seamless, effective, and engaging experience for all students. During the planning process, throughout the implementation, and since the creation of this integrated service center, we learned important lessons worth sharing with other Catholic colleges and universities.

CLARIFY THE GOAL

As individuals from different areas of the institution come together, the goal of the effort must be clear to all. Each member of the group brings his or her own important, although limited, perspective. Each must understand how their own experience and knowledge can contribute to achieving the goal, and that can only occur if the purpose of the effort is specific and clear. Therefore, as simple as this step seems, distribute the goal(s) in writing to the group. Review them at the first meeting and post them in a shared space. Remind the group of the ultimate goal(s) as often as needed to keep all moving in the right direction, to avoid tangents that devour time, and to accomplish the goal within a reasonable timeframe. It is easy for a group of thoughtful and dedicated individuals to become distracted as conversations progress and ideas are offered. Allow time for these cross-divisional conversations, as they can be very valuable in building and strengthening the relationship between SA and AA, but remain focused and respectful of time. Stakeholders will be more likely to agree to serve on a committee if they know they can rely on leadership to value their time and accomplish the goal.

COMMUNICATE AND EDUCATE

Be sure you are communicating with, and educating, stakeholders across divisions throughout the process. When appropriate, widely share the data, analysis, and conclusions. Offer updates on progress that are easily accessible. How important this is — and how wide you should cast the "information net" — depends on how many areas of the institution may be affected by the solution that is finally recommended. The effort to communicate and educate is particularly important if the solution is likely to require many individuals (including faculty) to change the way they currently do their work. Engage senior leadership where appropriate and request they include updates on the project in their communication with constituents. Otherwise, failure to communicate and educate, as well as competing priorities across the institution, may result in tremendous challenges during the implementation phase.

DEVELOP ALLIES

Develop allies while collaborating across divisions. Many of us serve on numerous committees. Be attentive to the language faculty use and the concerns they raise. Most are very interested in student success but are not necessarily aware of the role, or work, of their colleagues in SA. Be sure to present your work to faculty through both informal and formal channels. Cultivating relationships with allies across campus promotes a more holistic understanding of the student experience. The development of these critical relationships builds a strong bridge of respect that can form the foundation for an authentic and productive collaboration.

> "Cultivating relationships with allies across campus promotes a more holistic understanding of the student experience."

INVOLVE THE RIGHT PEOPLE

Bring creative individuals to the table who understand the issues under consideration and are willing and interested in learning more. Be sure to include new voices who will question the status quo alongside seasoned veterans who can influence others beyond the working group. Bring the expertise you need to the table and listen deeply. If you are working with a large group, break into smaller subcommittees and match people who have different perspectives, so their feedback and conclusions will incorporate those distinct elements of difference. Encourage many voices, even voices you know might be negative at first, because garnering support from those individuals is extremely important.

FIGHT AGAINST THE SILO CULTURE

Unfortunately, we often work in silos where decisions are made in isolation of the larger university community. Sometimes this is by choice, but more often it is by default. Silos in higher education are problematic for students, because students do not compartmentalize their lives in the same way we organize ourselves into divisions and departments. Our students and their families expect student-centered support services and they do not care who provides them or which budget pays for them. They simply expect effective services that are easy to access, and when this does not happen, they may question whether they belong and, worse, whether they should consider enrolling elsewhere. Student attrition should be everyone's concern. When we work in silos, we miss the opportunity to serve students holistically, a tradition in Catholic higher education. Catholic institutions are called to be attentive to the needs of students and deliver the highest level of care possible. We fail our students when our inability or unwillingness to authentically collaborate across divisions creates barriers that our students must work to overcome.

LISTEN TO STUDENTS

Creating a student-centered culture is the foundation for authentic collaboration. This can be done by engaging students in the conversation. Invite them into the dialogue by having student representation at every point in the process. This can take place as early as the idea generation meetings, all the way through the planning, marketing, and implementation processes.

BE PREPARED FOR THE FALLOUT

Change is hard. In higher education, change is often evolutionary rather than revolutionary, making rapid change even more difficult. Working in silos is conflict-avoidant behavior and complicates the ability of SA staff to foster authentic and effective collaboration among stakeholders. As SA professionals, it is helpful to become an expert in the relevant literature, review best practices at comparable institutions, and collect relevant data to support recommended changes. It is important to be strategic about how and when information is shared, because facts, rather than emotions, are often the most effective way to communicate change.

CONCLUSION

The authors highly value the collaborative relationship they have developed through their careers and through this initiative, but sustained change will not occur unless the collaborative mindset extends well beyond the individuals who initially fostered it. Innovation and creativity are necessary for our Catholic colleges and universities to thrive in such a competitive and volatile time in higher education. Creating departments with dual reporting lines, despite the complexity this creates for staff, budgeting, and technology systems, is an important step toward institutionalizing innovative change. Reinforcing our Catholic identity and values, by providing professional development opportunities grounded in community through collaboration between SA staff members and faculty members, is also essential. The Griff Center has been in place for two full years and issues continue to arise concerning who is responsible for what and how certain functions should be managed. From an administrative perspective, we continue to work to eliminate functional and cultural silos. From the student perspective, the Griff Center is a valuable, effective resource where issues are addressed and problems solved in a "one-stop-shop." Finally, institutional commitment to a student-centered approach must be deep and broad for collaborative initiatives to develop and succeed in lasting ways on campus.

Terri L. Mangione is the vice president for student affairs and Title IX coordinator, and Margaret Cain McCarthy is the vice president for academic affairs at Canisius College in Buffalo, New York.

CHAPTER 22

The Changing Role of the Athletic Director

Jay DeFruscio

Intercollegiate athletic programs have changed significantly in the last five years because of lucrative media rights deals, conference realignment, and multimillion-dollar corporate sponsorships, to name a few factors. As a result, college athletics has become big business and college athletic directors (ADs) are being asked to operate more as corporate CFOs than ever before. On a national level, "play for pay" and other student-athlete welfare issues dominate the discussions among college presidents and ADs and will continue to do so for the foreseeable future. The pressures to hire and pay the escalating coaches' salaries (especially in football and men's basketball), satisfy a rabid alumni fan base, and attend to the day-to-day administrative responsibilities of managing an athletic department have made the job much more complex than it was less than a decade ago. This is as true of Catholic institutions as it is of others.

College presidents are challenged with determining the role of the athletic department on their campuses. While athletic programs assist in recruiting students, generate revenues through ticket sales, merchandise, and fundraising, and serve as a source of publicity, the athletic department must be aligned with the mission of the university. As the leader of the department, the AD sets the tone both on and off the campus as it relates to running programs in support of the institution's Catholic mission.

MISSION AND THE DIRECTOR OF ATHLETICS

A mission statement is a declaration of "who we are" as an organization or institution. As a coach and athletic director at a Catholic institution, it was my responsibility to set the tone for my staff. How do we positively impact the lives of young people through mission? What sets us apart from non-Catholic institutions? How do we promote the uniqueness of our Catholic identity in recruiting staff and students? How does our department serve the underprivileged in our local community?

While it is true that the director of athletics is entrusted to lead the athletics department and has responsibility for creating a culture within the department that supports mission, it really is a team effort. When hired as the athletic director at

Wheeling Jesuit University, I made it a point to meet with the president and the director of campus ministry, among others on campus, to gain a better understanding of Jesuit education. Throughout my tenure, I found that working with campus ministry in hosting staff retreats was helpful to both new and returning staff.

The opportunity to gather intentionally, as a staff, with a spiritual focus is a unique opportunity for faith-based institutions. I found that mission-dedicated retreats or workshops worked well to uplift and motivate many of our athletic staff. Relationships among the staff were developed in simple ways through group community service projects, followed by reflection and sharing a meal.

How do we positively affect the lives of the student-athlete around mission?

Most successful teams have at least one thing in common: quality people committed to a shared goal. Human resource management is one of the biggest challenges an AD can face, because recruiting new staff members is critical to athletic department success. To help choose the best candidates, I involved many other campus departments in the screening and interviewing process, including faculty, student affairs, advancement, and campus ministry. We asked candidates what they knew about the university's mission and how they would model Catholic identity to the students. As a result, we built a department that was committed to community service and I was proud our coaches and student-athletes willingly embraced being a Jesuit mission of men and women committed to life, leadership, and most importantly, service to others.

Hiring excellent coaches committed to the mission of the institution mattered to me; choosing the right coaches helped create a departmental culture and expectations for supporting the Catholic mission of the university. Once a coach has been hired, part of the Athletic Director's job is not only assisting with the administrative transition, but also making sure the coach devotes time to the university's mission. I often accomplished this by working with the campus ministry staff or the institution's mission officer. As they settled into their new job, I often asked my coaches whether their programs were making progress, how they defined success, and in what ways they were helping their student-athletes grow. At a Catholic institution, commitment to the personal growth of our student-athletes is a vital part of our mission and of far more importance than wins and losses.

I do not want to imply that aspiring to excellence and winning are not important, because they are. However, compromising ethical values and principles to do so is not acceptable. I spent a great deal of time emphasizing the importance of building a winning culture based on foundations of hard work, selflessness, humility, and a willingness for individuals to sacrifice for the good of the team. If you build a winning culture, wins and championships will follow, as will recruits who want to be part of something great.

How do we positively affect the lives of young people through mission?

At many institutions, the athletic department is an extension of the admissions office. The athletic director sets the standards for the department and, as such, is a key member of the enrollment management team. Sharing personal experiences and focusing on values, especially the uncompromising integrity of our department, helped build a foundation of understanding and trust.

Prospective student-athletes choose a school for reasons different from those of the average prospective student. I made it a priority to meet with student-athletes and their parents when they visited campus. Each year we hosted an Athletic Open House at which prospects and families from all sports came together, on campus, on the same day. We involved the university's president, academic dean, dean of students, and director of campus ministry, as well as faculty, admissions representatives, and coaches. I always made it a point to speak about the mission of the university, making the connection between sports and spirituality. The event was held on a Sunday with the opportunity to attend Mass on campus. It was consistently one of our more successful recruiting events.

> "I always made it a point to speak about the mission of the university, making the connection between sports and spirituality."

How does our department serve the underprivileged in our community?

A commitment to service to the disadvantaged in the local community needs to be a priority for all athletic departments and, in most cases, is a key element of the mission statement. The athletic director, as the face of the department and the institution as well, is charged with actively leading and participating in all community service projects. To that end, we often began our school year with a prayer service for students, staff, and coaches in the chapel, with a coach and student sharing the benefits of leading an ethical, focused life grounded in a spiritual journey. Additionally, student-athletes and coaches participated in department-wide community service projects and team retreats. Finally, all were strongly encouraged to participate with the entire student body and, where possible, become actively engaged in leading others on campus and in the local community.

CONCLUSION

The job of a college director of athletics requires flexibility, a willingness to adapt to the changing environment, and ongoing evaluation in relation to the Catholic identity and university mission. As a practicing Catholic, my belief system is grounded in an unending commitment to the value and dignity of the human person. College athletics affords all in my care to develop their academic, athletic, social, and spiritual lives. These four dimensions of a Catholic university form the cornerstone of my work, as I strive to inspire young people in their pursuit to live a well-rounded life committed to service to others and to their community.

Jay DeFruscio is the associate commissioner at the Atlantic 10 Conference, headquartered in Newport News, Virginia.

CHAPTER 23

Working with Controversial Speakers and Events on a Catholic Campus

Todd A. Olson

A Catholic college or university lives with the tension created by two salient commitments: a commitment to live out and teach the Catholic mission and identity of the institution, and a commitment to be a modern American university, where the search for truth and the open exchange of ideas, even controversial ideas, is central to the academic experience. This tension is something student affairs professionals in a Catholic context need to navigate frequently.

Controversy is often related to issues of free speech and expression, especially when that expression is deemed offensive, inflammatory, or contrary to an institution's Catholic mission. It is in responding to controversy that our mission and identity are often tested, affirmed, questioned, and interpreted. For students, their awareness of mission at a Catholic institution is related to the elements of the institution they encounter on a regular basis (King & Herr, 2016). It is in how a college handles these tensions — in a student program, a speaker, or a policy decision — that salient teaching opportunities regarding mission emerge.

These tensions take many forms. They may be between the rights of the individual and the good of the community; between Catholic teachings and the unfettered exploration of ideas; or between freedom to express controversial views and ensuring a civil and orderly community for our students. We can find examples of this "tension balancing" in presidential messages about complex issues. University of Notre Dame President Rev. John Jenkins, CSC, wrote one such message in the wake of controversy about the play "The Vagina Monologues." He stated, "The challenge is not to do just one of these — or even to do both of them in parallel — but to promote academic freedom and affirm our Catholic character in a way that integrates the two and elevates both. This University was founded on the conviction that these goals are not just compatible, but essential, beneficial, and mutually reinforcing" (Jenkins, 2006).

To move from these conceptual tensions to issues of implementation, this chapter offers a set of practical guiding principles. Following that, a few examples of controversial situations illuminate how these principles might be applied in practice.

This set of principles is designed to frame thinking and guide action for student affairs administrators and the colleagues who work with them. Each institution has its own culture and norms, and the principles should be adapted as needed in that local context.

GUIDING PRINCIPLES FOR MANAGING CONTROVERSIAL ISSUES

It is important to facilitate conversations prior to a controversy. One of the most valuable roles student affairs leaders can play is to convene people around difficult topics on a proactive basis. Build a team of colleagues, within and beyond student affairs, who meet regularly to talk through emerging student issues. Even if it is one hour a month, this proactive approach is stronger than convening once a major problem has arisen. Depending on your campus culture, this team might include academic leaders, campus ministry, communications, alumni relations, and chief diversity officers. For this group and for others, tabletop exercises with scenarios of complex situations provide one structured way of sparking these conversations.

It is in the best interest of student affairs and our institutions that these issues not be managed solely within student affairs. It is also important that student affairs not be left out of, or marginalized in, these decisions. Results are most beneficial when student affairs leaders serve as conveners and question-framers, inviting in colleagues from other offices as appropriate.

It is vital to involve students directly in the tensions and decisions, when appropriate. There can be a powerful urge to resolve the situation and deliver a final response to students. This usually leads to resentment among students and closes off the potential learning and the sense of student "ownership" that can come from engaging students. We can point out the issues and the principles that are in tension and ask students for their ideas on how best to respond. Set clear expectations and guidelines for student input and ideas and how that information will be used to inform decision making.

There is real benefit in being aware of the interests and likely responses of external audiences and stakeholders. This may include your local ordinary, leaders of your sponsoring religious order, alumni, and parents. Consider when proactive communications with these stakeholders may be appropriate.

Policies provide a framework for decisions and for implementing our values. Make sure policies governing student organizations are clear and reference your Catholic mission and identity. Write policies that acknowledge and balance the tensions described above.

It is vital to understand and articulate distinctions among the following hosts or conveners of speakers and programs:

1. The university, the president's office, or an administrative unit may invite speakers and may bestow honorary degrees. This is a place where the invitation can imply direct endorsement of a speaker's views.

2. An academic department or program generally enjoys a level of academic freedom to invite speakers with a wide range of views.

3. Student organizations may also enjoy a level of freedom to invite controversial speakers.

"Ruling out a controversial speaker or program after it is proposed is a very challenging task."

With all conveners, it is important to seek clarity about what the guiding policies and principles are before a given speaker is invited or a program is planned. Ruling out a controversial speaker or program after it is proposed is a very challenging task. It is far preferable to communicate clear guidance, and encourage appropriate consultation, in advance.

Finally, it is valuable to include information about controversial topics and Catholic mission and identity in orientations for new faculty members, student affairs staff, and student leaders. The *Principles of Good Practice for Student Affairs at Catholic Colleges and Universities* (2010) is an excellent resource for putting our mission and identity into practice. The examples below offer a starting point for testing out these principles in complex situations.

EXAMPLES FOR DISCUSSION

1. Students petition to form a group called "Feminists United for Change" and list "advocating for reproductive justice" as one of eight goals for their group. The other seven goals address women's full participation in campus organizations, the political process, and the life of the university.

2. A student organization invites a speaker to campus who is an atheist and is known for mocking organized religion in all her speeches. A group of Catholic student leaders on campus ask the administration to rescind the invitation, because this speaker does not respect the mission of the college.

3.   Your local bishop is invited to deliver the commencement address. During the year, he has been vocal about defending the traditional definition of marriage. A group of students informs you that they plan an active protest during his speech, because his views are oppressive to LGBTQ students.

4.   The campus career center posts internship opportunities for students each year. A local nonprofit wants to post an opportunity for a "transgender health care intern" to work in a local clinic with patients going through a gender transition. After a career center staff member posts this opening, a group of parents and alumni organize on social media and put pressure on you to take down this posting, which they describe as "a slap in the face of our Catholic identity."

Todd A. Olson is vice president for student affairs at Georgetown University in Washington, DC.

REFERENCES

Jenkins, J. (2006). Closing Statement on Academic Freedom and Catholic Character. Retrieved from http://president.nd.edu/writings-addresses/2006-writings/statements-on-academic-freedom/closing-statement.

King, J. & Herr, A. (2016). "Does Catholic Identity Affect Students?" *Journal of Catholic Higher Education*, 34(2).

PRINCIPLE FOUR

*Creates opportunities for students
to experience, reflect upon, and act from
a commitment to justice, mercy,
and compassion, and in light of Catholic
social teaching to develop respect and
responsibility for all, especially
those most in need.*

CHAPTER 24 Educating for Justice and Compassion: **139**
Catholic Social Teaching and the Work of
Student Affairs

Thomas Mogan, Boston College

CHAPTER 25 *Laudato Si* and Its Relevance for   **145**
Student Affairs

*Rev. Dennis E. Tamburello, OFM,
Siena College*

CHAPTER 24

Educating for Justice and Compassion: Catholic Social Teaching and the Work of Student Affairs

Thomas Mogan

INTRODUCTION

For professionals charged with the formation of students in the Catholic tradition, an understanding of Catholic Social Teaching is vital to the work of student affairs in Catholic higher education. Catholic Social Teaching (CST) is characterized by the United States Conference of Catholic Bishops as a "rich treasure of wisdom about building a just society and living lives of holiness amidst the challenges of modern society" (USCCB, n.d.). Indeed, much of our work in student affairs is dedicated to supporting students in their quest to live lives of meaning, purpose, and passion. Invoking a foundational principle of Ignatian spirituality, student affairs professionals at Catholic colleges and universities should seek to empower students to "go set the world aflame."

Much has been written on the benefits and best practices of service and service learning programs on college campuses. Less well understood and practiced is how to turn our gaze inward and practice principles of CST on our own campuses with students and other members of our campus communities. If Catholic higher education's focus is to be on formative education, greater attention should be paid to the campus community as a laboratory for the kind of civic engagement to which we hope our students aspire. Opportunities for action and reflection are essential to help students grow in this tradition. Some of the best practices found within these programs will be explored below. The move beyond a traditional model of service to one rooted in social justice can be more complicated; however, it can also provide meaningful opportunities to partner with academic programs.

CATHOLIC SOCIAL TEACHING DEFINED

Catholic Social Teaching refers to the collected wisdom on political, economic, and cultural issues that has been articulated through a series of official Church documents. These documents have been issued by popes, bishops, and other Church leaders and represent efforts by the Church to interpret modern social issues through the lens of the Catholic Intellectual Tradition. While there is no firm consensus on the precise definition of CST, the United States Conference of Catholic Bishops has identified seven themes of Catholic Social Teaching (USCCB, n.d.). These seven principles are:

- Life and Dignity of the Human Person

- Call to Family, Community, and Participation

- Protection of Rights and Responsibilities

- Option for the Poor and Vulnerable

- The Dignity of Work and the Rights of Workers

- Solidarity

- Care for God's Creation

- Applying CST Principles in Student Affairs

The clearest example of how student affairs professionals incorporate these principles into their work is through service programs and other programs that educate for justice and compassion. The most effective and successful programs are ones that provide significant opportunities for students to reflect on their service. Students should be encouraged to consider their service work in at least two dimensions. First, students should be given the opportunity and space to contemplate the ways in which their service affects them as persons and the role of their faith. Through service, students can learn a great deal about themselves and how they relate to others and may, thereby, discover their strengths and find passion and purpose in their lives. Second, reflection provides the opportunity for students to see how their faith can be strengthened through their work. The act of performing caring and compassionate service may allow students to see the work of God in others and themselves.

The process of reflection can also inspire students to move from an orientation of service to one of advocacy for social justice. Structured reflection experiences should encourage students to think beyond the processing of their own thoughts and feelings by asking them to focus on larger issues of social justice. To assist students in placing their service experiences in a broader context, student affairs professionals need to educate students about the underlying causes of injustice, as well as about the principles and practices of social justice advocacy.

One of the most effective ways in which Catholic colleges and universities expose their students to social justice issues is through domestic and international service immersion experiences. These experiences have the power to change the lives and career trajectories of our students. They are designed to take students out of their comfort zones and place them into situations where they are asked to confront the realities of people who are different from themselves. At times, these experiences can spark a movement or embolden students to want to do more.

The story of Water for Waslala is an excellent example of how a service experience can lead to positive and long-lasting change. Matt Nespoli, Nora Reynolds, and seven other Villanova University students traveled to Waslala, Nicaragua in 2002 on a two-week service immersion program. Matt, Nora, and the other students were deeply affected by the poverty and lack of infrastructure in Waslala, as well as the beauty and warmth of the people they visited. The people of Waslala indicated that their most urgent need was to access clean drinking water. Matt and Nora returned home committed to finding a way to end the Waslala water crisis and, in 2004, they created Water for Waslala (WfW) to do so. Villanova University's engineering school has partnered with the group to provide technical assistance, while the units of student affairs and campus ministry have supported their efforts to establish a student organization and assist in their fundraising efforts. Since its inception, WfW has provided 2,500 Waslalans with clean drinking water.

> "The process of reflection can also inspire students to move from an orientation of service to one of advocacy for social justice."

As the case of Water for Waslala demonstrates, some of the most successful programs that focus on social justice involve creative partnerships with academic departments and programs. Catholic colleges and universities should continue to sponsor and develop living learning communities and other academic experiences that focus on combining service with educational components. One of the oldest and most successful programs that focuses on combining CST and service is the PULSE Program at Boston College. Started in 1970, the mission of the PULSE Program is to "educate our students about social injustice by putting them into direct contact with marginalized populations and social change organizations and by encouraging discussion on classic and contemporary works of philosophy and theology" (About PULSE, n.d.). As part of the PULSE Program, Boston College students take a 12-credit, yearlong, core-level course in philosophy and theology titled "Person and Social Responsibility." In addition to classroom reflection and discussion, carefully selected field placements in after-school programs, youth work, corrections, shelters, literacy programs, domestic violence centers, health clinics, housing programs, and other areas become the context in which students forge a critical and compassionate perspective both on society and themselves. A 2010 study by Boston University researchers found that students participating in the PULSE Program demonstrated statistically significant shifts toward an understanding of poverty that emphasized structural causes over individual causes (Seider, Rabinowicz, & Gillmor, 2010).

Beyond service programs, opportunities to raise awareness about social justice issues and to advocate for social change can be found within the realm of student organizations. Catholic Relief Services has worked with partner institutions — including Villanova University and Boston College — to develop Ambassador programs that raise awareness about global issues. Students involved in the Ambassador program become educated on issues such as global poverty, immigration, human trafficking, and food security. The organization then seeks to raise awareness about these issues and encourages students to act to support their advocacy efforts.

While advocacy and social justice work is needed and helps develop students into global leaders for others, Catholic colleges and universities need to consider ways we can work to build and support the common good on our own campuses. Today's Catholic colleges and universities are complex environments and thus in many ways are laboratories of civic life. By inviting students to be part of the internal dynamics of university life, and by encouraging them to reflect critically on those dynamics, the university can help prepare them for life in a complex, globalized world. Key to this invitation to students is providing opportunities to engage students in facilitated, structured dialogue.

Student affairs administrators can play a vital role in advocating for the needs of students. Yet, as the recent wave of protests on campuses across the country demonstrates, students often do not feel heard, or listened to, by college and university administrators. Central to our mission as advocates for students, student affairs professionals should foster opportunities to seek ways to encourage dialogue between students and the administration. Dialogue provides opportunities to listen and to share what is happening, and allows for experiences to be heard and felt. Rooted in the principles of CST, the Catholic mission of our institutions calls us to listen closely to the voices of the marginalized on our campuses.

In adopting a preferential option for the poor, student life professionals at Catholic colleges and universities should focus concern on economic disparities and inequalities found on our own campuses. We should assess how support to under-resourced students, who may feel less of a sense of belonging on campus, is provided. While the classroom can be an economic equalizer, other experiences outside the classroom are, effectively, economic discriminators; students on our campus may feel that there exists a system of inequality when it comes to co-curricular experiences. Students who must hold jobs in addition to attending classes are often at a disadvantage in terms of feeling a part of the campus community. Campus policies and procedures should be evaluated and assessed to ensure that all students, regardless of economic means, are offered the opportunity to fully experience the rich and transformative curricular and co-curricular experiences that our institutions provide.

In addition to addressing the economic inequalities among our student body, administrators at Catholic colleges and universities are uniquely positioned to demonstrate concern for those lower-paid employees who work at our institutions. These employees, often found in the areas of dining services and facilities management, should be acknowledged by student affairs professionals at the various events that bring together the campus community. Students should be encouraged to show appreciation to these hard-working people for their important contributions to the quality of campus life. For example, residence hall professionals can work with the facilities staff to foster a closer connection to students in their building. This could be done through passive programming (bulletin boards) or through a social event where students and staff can share their stories.

The tradition of CST has much to offer student affairs professionals. To be most effective on today's Catholic campuses, the application of CST's tenets must be in dialogue with the mission and charism of the institution. In the spirit of the discourse espoused above, professional development opportunities available to staff should promote the principles of CST and provide a means of fostering their application on our campuses.

Thomas Mogan is associate vice president/dean of students at Boston College in Boston, Massachusetts.

REFERENCES

Boston College. (n.d.). About PULSE. Retrieved from http://www.bc.edu/schools/cas/pulse/about.html.

Seider, S. C., Rabinowicz, S. A., & Gillmor, S. C. (2010). "Changing American College Students' Conceptions of Poverty through Community Service Learning." *Analyses of Social Issues and Public Policy* 11(1), 105-126.

United States Conference of Catholic Bishops. (n.d.). Seven themes of Catholic social teaching. Retrieved from http://www.usccb.org/beliefs-and-teachings/what-we-believe/catholic-social-teaching/seven-themes-of-catholic-social-teaching.cfm.

CHAPTER 25

Laudato Sí and Its Relevance for Student Affairs

Dennis E. Tamburello, OFM

When we think of the missions of our Catholic colleges and universities, the first thing that probably does not come to mind is their divine mandate to protect and care for the earth. We often focus — appropriately, of course — on how we relate to God and to one another, stressing prayer, service to others, and working for justice for all of God's people. Yet, at the risk of stating the obvious, every one of our institutions exists in a natural context. Many of our campuses incorporate extensive tracts of land. In the course of fulfilling our mission, we consume valuable resources in lighting and heating our buildings, printing course materials, providing food and water, and transporting students on field and service trips.

More and more, the question of sustainable use of the world's resources has become pressing in our homes, schools, and businesses. Pope Francis's encyclical *Laudato Sí: On Care for Our Common Home*, offers us a strong and articulate framework for raising and addressing the issue of environmental responsibility in these contexts. While its insights can be argued intellectually in academic courses, it is in student affairs where *Laudato Sí* can perhaps have a greater impact on the college and university campus, because its arguments relate to almost everything we do both inside and outside the classroom. The purpose of this chapter is to show how the theology of *Laudato Sí* can be used to promote a more sustainable campus and world.

THEOLOGICAL THEMES

Several theological themes are prominent in *Laudato Sí*. One of the most central is that everything is interconnected. Indeed, Pope Francis not only makes a connection between environmental and social justice, but also connects ecology to politics, personal morality, world peace, the Holy Family, the Trinity, the saints, and the sacraments. Many of these themes converge in the figure of St. Francis of Assisi, whose vision of the created world shines forth in his famous *Canticle of the Creatures*.

Pope Francis addresses his encyclical to all people of good will. He particularly hopes that his message will resonate with young people, who already have been sensitized to environmental issues (10; all references are to section numbers). At the same time, he unapologetically grounds his arguments in belief in God. Over and over again, the Pope insists that there is Something (nature) and Someone (God) bigger than ourselves, to which and to whom we are responsible (67 and 68).

One of the main corollaries of this belief is the notion of the common good: "the sum of those conditions of social life which allow social groups and their individual members relatively thorough and ready access to their own fulfillment" (156). The idea of the common good implies that we must have respect for creation that goes beyond utilitarianism, i.e., what the world can provide for us.

Pope Francis is not opposed to seeing human beings as having a special place in creation — indeed, he affirms this strongly in his chapter on the Gospel of Creation (81). But this special status carries with it the responsibility to be stewards of creation, to nurture and protect the environment. For other creatures, too, are important and have a value independent of what they can provide for us. If humans should not be treated as mere objects, neither should the rest of God's creation. As the Holy Father puts it, "No creature is superfluous" (84). Thus, Pope Francis tries to create a balance between a legitimate anthropocentrism and an egalitarian environmental ethic.

One of the greatest obstacles to what Pope Francis calls an "integral ecology" (first mentioned in section 10) is consumerism, which leads to selfishness, individualism, and disregard for the limitations of the world's resources (203-204). In its place, he proposes a simpler lifestyle in which "less is more" (222), and an economy that serves the needs of all people, not just the wealthy. Francis sees consumerism as a major factor in the marginalization of the poor, who do not have access to many of the luxuries enjoyed by the affluent and who suffer disproportionately the effects of environmental degradation.

Pope Francis calls for both personal conversion and social conversion. We need to take both individual and communal steps toward a sustainable ecological lifestyle. He insists that ecological conversion is not "optional" or "secondary" (217). Just as the Church needed to recognize the scriptural call to social justice, which it has done in its social teaching over the past 100-plus years, so now it needs to recognize the scriptural call to care for the earth. This emphasis on the care of creation has always been in Scripture, but it was ignored for many centuries, until the modern industrial age brought us to ecological crisis.

PRACTICAL APPLICATIONS

There is much more that could be said about the encyclical, and it is most worthy of a close and careful reading to mine its riches. But the remainder of this chapter will draw some practical implications of the encyclical for those who work in higher education. At one point, Pope Francis calls for a "new way of thinking" (215) about the world. Of all the places where young people should be exposed to new ways of thinking, it is most appropriate on Catholic college and university campuses. What we need is not only a new way of thinking, but also a new way of acting. Pope Francis speaks of instilling "good habits" (212). This is something that student affairs is uniquely qualified to do.

> "What we need is not only a new way of thinking, but also a new way of acting."

From an affirmative and proactive position, student affairs professionals can encourage the change in lifestyle that Pope Francis challenges us to undertake. This is often easy to do, as many students are already attuned to respecting and protecting the environment. We can encourage students to purchase fair trade products, to buy "green," to recycle, and to compost. We can urge them to respect their own bodies, as Pope Francis so eloquently stated: "Learning to accept our body, to care for it and to respect its fullest meaning, is an essential element of any genuine human ecology" (155). We can train our community living staffs so that they can offer programs that inform their peers about the crucial issues surrounding sustainability.

Often, the best way for students to have a significant effect on the care of creation is to join a student club or organization devoted to some aspect of environmentalism. Student affairs professionals should promote this kind of involvement. Where a club or local organization does not exist, the student activities office can assist students in starting one on their campus.

From a more responsive position, we periodically encounter vandalism on our campuses. We have often addressed this problem by saying to students: "Don't do to a campus building something you wouldn't do to your own home." In light of *Laudato Sí*, maybe the message we send should be wider in scope: "Don't do anything to hurt our common home, which is not just the campus, but the entire world." Student conduct sanctions for vandalism might best be the assignment of an environmental service, like cleaning up a local park.

On the issue of consumerism, there is often no better way to get students thinking about this than taking them on a service trip to an economically disadvantaged or even destitute community. Students and chaperones alike are often transformed by meeting people for whom less truly is more, who live without the superfluity of goods, and yet are often extraordinarily generous and kind. While we do not want to glorify destitute poverty, the poor in their simplicity have much to teach us.

Pope Francis presents a vision that offers a goldmine of opportunities for student affairs staff. Faced with an overwhelming environmental crisis, the Holy Father expresses hope, recognizing that "humans are capable of rising above themselves and choosing what is good" (205). Many of our students (though certainly not all) — and many of us who are student affairs professionals — have been raised with a level of affluence that the vast majority of the world's population will never experience. We would do well to take Pope Francis's words to heart and open ourselves to the challenge of building a more just, peaceful, and sustainable world.

Rev. Dennis E. Tamburello, OFM, is professor of religious studies and Friar in Residence at Siena College in Loudonville, New York.

REFERENCE

Pope Francis. (2015). Encyclical Letter *Laudato Sí* of the Holy Father Francis on Care for Our Common Home. The Holy See: Vatican Press.

PRINCIPLE FIVE

Challenges students to high standards of personal behavior and responsibility through the formation of character and virtues.

CHAPTER 26 College Student Discipline and   151
               Catholic Identity

               Andrew Skotnicki, Manhattan College,
               and Colette McCarrick Geary, College of
               St. Scholastica

CHAPTER 27 Sexual Misconduct: Title IX and   157
               Catholic Mission

               Kathleen J. Byrnes, Villanova University

CHAPTER 28 Threat Assessment, Risk Management,   161
               and Catholic Mission

               Marisa R. Randazzo, Georgetown University

CHAPTER 26

College Student Discipline and Catholic Identity

Andrew Skotnicki and Colette McGarrick Geary

The mission of virtually any institution of higher education references the creation of the optimal conditions for student learning and personal development. This is no less true on Catholic campuses where a host of earnest and important conversations and innovations have been introduced concerning Catholic identity. The college student disciplinary process provides a unique opportunity for Catholic colleges to espouse values that set our campuses apart from other institutions of higher learning.

Disciplinary codes on college campuses make salient community standards for conduct and may serve as a concrete and valuable instrument for promoting a campus climate conducive to the educational mission. However, the responsibility for oversight of college student discipline has become an extraordinarily complex matter. The contemporary practice paradigm has been shaped by an evolving and complex understanding of the relationship between universities and their students. Various factors have played a role, including: significant decisions by federal and state courts, the apparent similitude of processes for college investigations and hearings to criminal proceedings, and the challenge of responding to evolving regulatory issues (Gehring, 2001). The resulting tension that must be resolved in each disciplinary encounter concerns the optimal means to restore integrity to a *community* that has been fractured, in some way, by the actions of an *individual* member. In an excessively legalistic or punitive culture, student conduct processes may potentially serve as alienating and judgmental experiences that turn the intended intimacy of a campus encounter into an extension of the adversarial spirit of our courtrooms and, to an ever-growing extent, our society, thus significantly detracting from the laudable goals of personal and educational growth.

Catholic institutions are challenged not only to be accountable to external and internal cultural pressures, but also to preserve right relationships with students in the light of our faith. The philosophy and process for managing student discipline provide ripe occasions for the faithful pursuit of the collective ideal to form "an authentic human community animated by the spirit of Christ" (USCCB, 2006, p. 58). Accordingly, when initiating staff members, it is essential to communicate that compliance with *due process* and related requirements constitute a necessary, but not sufficient, condition. We can draw upon our rich tradition of Catholic thought to advance a theologically grounded vision of student discipline that will refresh our vocational zeal in this challenging work. To that end, we offer three guiding principles that should inform a Catholic approach to student discipline: forgiveness, accompaniment, and humility.

FORGIVENESS

Judicial staff face the inherent risk of acquiring a biased view of the student because of a disproportional attentiveness to a specific poor choice or untoward event. When we meet a student as "the accused," one must fight the tendency to allow a single event to define our view of him or her. We believe that there is a concrete way to avoid this alienating posture that, despite the good intentions of the administrator, can further isolate the student or, worse, stigmatize him or her due to the disintegrative effects of labeling theory. While forgiveness is an essential virtue for Christians, it is also the most compelling logic for a Catholic approach to wrongdoing.

Sin can best be described as the willful rupture of relationship. In our "legal" culture, this strikes us as archaic or naïve, but for the first thousand years of the Christian experience that was precisely how sin was understood: as an act that harmed the relationship between the offender and victim and, a *fortiori*, between the offender and God (Brague, 2008; Favazza, 1988). The task of the sacrament of penance was to restore the damaged relationship by means of acknowledgment of fault, contrition, and absolution. Penance was the response of the penitent to the gratuitous and forgiving love of God, a penance not imposed by God (for there are no conditions upon God's love) but ideally brought by the penitent upon him or herself. Recent theological treatises have reminded us of this positive dynamic (Jones, 1995, Rahner, 1982).

In this framework, there is no positive good that can come from imposing punishments upon students who have committed behavioral infractions. They have already broken relationships; they are alienated; and deep within, they are aware of their isolation and loneliness. The question, then, is how to create the conditions for them to allow the pains of separation to rise and to accompany them as they seek ways to respond to the harm they have done to themselves and to others. An example of this concerns a young man found responsible for misconduct who revealed that his primary motivation for succumbing to peer pressure was his hope that, by joining in, "maybe these guys would call me when they are going to the gym." Recognizing his deep loneliness and resulting vulnerability, forgiveness is articulated through a sanction carefully planned to enable him the opportunity to access a welcoming and affirming peer group. In this case, assigning service hours on a popular campus ministry project enabled him to forge healthy friendships and become socially connected. By protecting the privacy of this assignment, he was not stigmatized in this new social context. Sanctions that facilitate this kind of movement toward wholeness and unity must consider the unique needs and circumstances of the individual's transgression and any challenges they may face in achieving reintegration.

ACCOMPANIMENT

The openness to being in relationship with each student is a vital pathway to the best understanding of them in the fullest context of

> "We can draw upon our rich tradition of Catholic thought to advance a theologically grounded vision of student discipline."

their individualism and their life story. The metaphorical stance of accompaniment can be visualized by staff as a "standing next to, and looking with the student at their situation," not a "looking down upon." It is a way of saying: *I'm here with you in this challenging moment, and I want to support you in what you must do to become more fully integrated.* In practical terms, this stance implies a commitment to the person and to forgoing the far more convenient and, at least from a retributive standpoint, satisfying resolution of the conflictual situation in something akin to a zero-sum equation. While the latter approach mirrors our adversarial judicial system and many elements of our popular culture, it once again pales in comparison to the Catholic sacramental tradition wherein no offense can be seen as stigmatizing. Excommunication in the early Church was both a summons to prayer, self-examination, and penance on the part of the wrongdoer and a summons to the Christian community to accompany the penitent as he or she went through the difficult and painful process of facing the harm done to the self, to human relationships, and to one's relationship with God (McNeill, 1951, Poschmann, 1964).

A poignant example is found in a freshman who seemed to be having trouble adjusting to college, appearing on several incident reports within the first few weeks of school. It was soon learned that he was a defendant in a manslaughter case stemming from a prom night accident that left one friend dead and others injured. As his trial date approached, a faculty member, who had experience as a prison chaplain, stepped in to accompany the student through the next stage as he prepared to be separated from the college and face years of confinement. For this student, giving voice to the profound emotional movements within required an attentive listener to hear and be present to his suffering. Our response to student misconduct should mirror the accompaniment of one on a penitential journey.

HUMILITY

As students first encounter the disciplinary process, they are likely to respond in ways that are consistent with prior personal experiences of judgment or correction. Without knowing the starting place, the Catholic administrator must begin any encounter with profound respect for the great dignity of the human person, which helps to frame all that follows. Judging a student as uncooperative will prompt a different staff response than will one assessing a student as situationally vulnerable — and only the latter will lead to attempts to make the student feel safe. Appropriate humility is expressed when staff are duly conscious of avoiding any tendencies toward hasty assumptions or heavy handedness in their oversight of even routine disciplinary interactions.

For a student who is deeply anguished over a poor decision, reframing the situation from the specific event to an expression of the frailty of our human condition may engender feelings of trust between student and staff. Statements such as, "I have been in your shoes. I have made my own share of decisions that I sorely regretted" can be powerful tools to build relationship and are not meant to be rhetorical. The heart of our spiritual tradition is the call to personal holiness and to suffer the necessary failures we all make as we try to diminish our egos and submit wholeheartedly to the guidance of the Holy Spirit. The only consistently truthful stance for the Christian, in light of the person we are called to be and the person we have in fact become, is humility — a humility that binds us in solidarity with all the students we are graced to serve, particularly those who have failed to live as they know they ought.

In witnessing the way a given college approaches student discipline, members of the community will learn something about the Catholic perspective on what it means to be human, especially as this concerns our moral and ethical decisions. The student discipline process plays an indispensable role in contributing to the culture of the campus and to the priorities that are reflective of an authentically Catholic community of learning.

Andrew Skotnicki is professor of religious studies at Manhattan College in New York City. Colette McCarrick Geary is the president of College of St. Scholastica in Duluth, Minnesota.

REFERENCES

Brague, R. (2008). *The Law of God*. (L.G. Cochrane, Trans.). Chicago: University of Chicago Press.

Favazza, J. (1988). *The Order of Penitents*. Collegeville, MN: Liturgical Press.

Gehring, D. (2001). "The Objectives of Student Discipline and the Process That's Due: Are They Compatible?" *Bowling Green State University: Higher Education and Student Affairs Faculty Publications* 38(4), 466-481.

Jones, L. G. (1995). *Embodying Forgiveness*. Grand Rapids, MI: Eerdmans.

McNeill, J. T. (1951). *A History of the Cure of Souls*. New York: Harper & Row.

Poschmann, B. (1964). *Penance and the Anointing of the Sick*. (Courtney, F., Trans.). New York: Herder & Herder.

Rahner, K. (1982). "Penance in the Early Church." *Theological Investigations* 15. (L. Swain, Trans.). New York: Crossroad.

United States Conference of Catholic Bishops. (2006). *Catholic Identity in Our Colleges and Universities: A Collection of Defining Documents*. Washington, DC: USCCB.

CHAPTER 27

Sexual Misconduct:
Title IX and Catholic Mission

Kathleen J. Byrnes

In 2011, the U.S. Department of Education's Office for Civil Rights (OCR) renewed its call through a *Dear Colleague* letter to colleges and universities to be more vigilant in preventing and addressing sexual violence on campus. Since then, virtually every school has reexamined, and in most cases reinvigorated, both its educational and procedural responses to sexual misconduct on campus. The campuses of Catholic colleges and universities are fortunate, because their Catholic identities lend tremendous support to their response to instances of sexual misconduct. By definition, Catholic campuses seek to foster and maintain communities of care and respect, where the sacredness and dignity of each human person is held in the highest regard. In addition, Principle Five of the *Principles of Good Practice* calls Catholic colleges and universities to "challenge students to high standards of personal behavior and responsibility through the formation of character and virtue." Thus, Principle Five also provides the frame for implementing comprehensive policies and educational programs that "seek to eliminate sexual misconduct, prevent its recurrence, and address its effects."

OCR GUIDANCE AND VAWA AMENDMENTS

Title IX of the Civil Rights Act (1972) prohibits educational programs receiving federal funding from discriminating on the basis of sex. Relatedly, colleges and universities have long had provisions in their codes of student conduct prohibiting sexual assault and other sexual misconduct behaviors. However, these behaviors typically were understood as violations of the code of conduct and of state law, not necessarily viewed as civil rights violations under Title IX. The 2011 *Dear Colleague* letter clarified that sexual misconduct on college campuses potentially constitutes a Title IX violation if the allegations of sexual misconduct are not responded to appropriately by the school. In 2015, amendments to the Violence Against Women Act (VAWA) took effect, further delineating expected elements to be included in a school's sexual misconduct policy and broadening the mandatory crimes reported by colleges and universities pursuant to the Clery Act. Schools must now include reported incidents of dating violence, domestic violence, and stalking that occur on Clery geography, among other things. Policies must also include clear definitions of these behaviors.

The *Dear Colleague* letter, along with guidance arising out of OCR investigations and the VAWA amendments, has led schools to review and revise policies and procedures. To briefly summarize, updated policies should include:

- Provisions regarding investigation of all allegations made by a community member, consistent with the wishes of the reporting person, when possible.

- Timely warnings issued on campus when helpful to keep the campus safe from additional harm when a report is made.

- "Preponderance of the evidence" standard of proof in campus disciplinary proceedings.

- The right to an advisor, during campus disciplinary proceedings, for each of the students involved, of each student's choosing.

- Completion of the investigation and proceeding within 60 days of the allegations, absent unusual circumstances.

- Appropriate training required for those sitting on campus disciplinary panels.

- Equal rights to appeal for each of the parties.

- Inclusion of dating violence, domestic violence, and stalking in sexual misconduct policies and Clery reporting.

- Designation of a Title IX coordinator and the publication of a Title IX Notice.

- Proactive and comprehensive approach to training and educational programs on sexual misconduct and other included offenses across all campus constituencies, i.e., students, faculty, and staff.

- Special mindfulness of bystander intervention training regarding sexual assault and other sexual misconduct, and of appropriate academic accommodation and other interim measures for students who have reported such behaviors.

- Requirement that "responsible employees" report incidents of sexual violence to the Title IX coordinator or other person designated by the institution, where responsible employees are those who have the authority, or who a student could reasonably believe has the authority, to address and/or report an allegation of sexual misconduct.

In addition to these suggestions, the White House has instituted a campaign called *1 is 2 Many*. This campaign focuses on sexual violence and offers many helpful resources. Its message is well aligned with Principle Five, and readers are referred to it for additional guidance.

PRACTICAL IMPLICATIONS FOR CATHOLIC CAMPUSES

To comply with the law is obviously paramount, but sexual violence is not only about the law; it is about taking care of students and doing the right thing. Catholic campuses are called to: do the right things to support students who report; do the right things in the processes that seek to hold students accountable when they have acted badly; and do the right things by constantly being mindful that Catholic institutions are called to enhance the growth and development of students in mind, body, and spirit, i.e., their character and virtue.

How must schools seek to prevent and respond to these incidents in a way that is reflective of Catholic values? First, each institution needs to establish policies that comply with the law, highlighted above. Second, schools need to ensure that their practices (a) exemplify Principle Five in their work with students, (b) respect and support the students involved, including the respondents, and (c) take additional steps to prevent the recurrence of sexual misconduct and redress its effects. Here is a checklist of possible strategies to address these three goals:

> "Empower students to be bystanders who effectively intervene when danger of any kind is lurking."

1. Focus on student training that anticipates students' continuing development of their values and behavior regarding sexual activity, alcohol and other drug use, and their understanding of consent. Training should provide a venue for conversations with students, not just about sexual misconduct, but about broader issues such as intimacy and respect; about what they or their friends can do to make sure they are not doing harm to another. Empower students to be bystanders who effectively intervene when danger of any kind is lurking. Studies show that bystander intervention is a powerful strategy to prevent many problems, including sexual violence.

2. Offer and well publicize the resources available to reporting students, including offices such as campus ministry and counseling centers. Clearly specify which are confidential and which are not, options for how and to whom to report, and what to expect when reporting. Clear information communicates respect for the survivor, allowing the student to make an informed choice. And ensure that the people identified as campus resources are trained to treat any reporting person with the care and dignity consistent with Catholic identity.

3. Provide support to the accused student, i.e., the respondent. Typically, respondents also are students and warrant respectful treatment. Designate a faculty or staff member outside the disciplinary process who can share information with a respondent about the process, along with the availability of the counseling center and other support. This designee should not be the advisor to the student in a disciplinary proceeding, because the cases are too complex and nuanced, but the designee can offer information to help the respondent make good decisions in managing the process. In addition, those conducting the investigation must remember to maintain the presumption of innocence, to treat the respondent with respect, and to refrain from pre-judging the outcome of the matter during the investigation. This approach not only complies with Title IX but also affords the respondent the same respect offered the reporting student.

CONCLUSION

In short, given their own mission of respect for the sacredness of each human person, Catholic colleges and universities should welcome the increased attention to issues of sexual violence initiated by the Office for Civil Rights under Title IX. Catholic values suggest a holistic response, focusing on the protection and moral development of students, where care and respect for the inherent dignity of all prevail.

Kathleen J. Byrnes is associate vice president for student life at Villanova University in Villanova, Pennsylvania.

REFERENCES

Clery Center for Security on Campus. *VAWA Amendments to Clery.* 2015. Retrieved from http://clerycenter.org/article/vawa-amendments-clery.

The White House. *1 Is 2 Many.* Retrieved from https://www.whitehouse.gov/1is2many.

U.S. Department of Education, Office for Civil Rights. *Dear Colleague* Letter. April 4, 2011. Retrieved from http://www2.ed.gov/about/offices/list/ocr/letters/colleague-201104.html.

CHAPTER 28

Threat Assessment, Risk Management, and Catholic Mission

Marisa R. Randazzo

In the wake of the campus shootings at Virginia Tech in 2007, U.S. federal agencies, state taskforces, professional associations, and other respected entities have released reports on campus safety and violence prevention. One common theme across these numerous reports is that colleges and universities in the United States should create and operate behavioral threat assessment teams in order to prevent violence (IACLEA, 2008). This recommendation was echoed in the American National Standard for higher education risk analysis, approved by the American National Standards Institute (ANSI) in 2010, which strongly suggested that colleges and universities should implement campus threat assessment teams (ASME Innovative Technologies Institute, LLC, 2010). In the opinion of some commentators, campus threat assessment is not merely a recommendation but an emerging standard of care, at least for U.S. colleges and universities (Nolan, Randazzo, & Deisinger, 2011). The threat assessment model is not only broadly recommended as best practice for preventing campus violence, but also now required by law for higher education institutions in Connecticut, Illinois, and Virginia.

In the setting of Catholic colleges and universities, threat assessment programs can both prevent potential violence and also support Catholic educational missions. Catholic schools are uniquely primed to care about their students in and out of the classroom. As such, threat assessment work is directly related to the underlying missions of Catholic institutions of higher education, particularly the missions of care of the whole person and honoring the sacredness of each person. Catholic colleges and universities are places where the community is founded in the Gospel value of loving one's self and others and of putting others first; the principles of behavioral threat assessment fit well within the mission of Catholic higher education, in terms of keeping everyone cared for and safe. This chapter reviews components of current best practices in campus threat assessment and the manner in which an effective campus threat assessment program can operate at Catholic colleges and universities.

THREAT ASSESSMENT: WHAT IT IS AND WHAT IT IS NOT

Behavioral threat assessment (also known simply as "threat assessment") is a prevention-focused model that has been used successfully by federal law enforcement for several decades in efforts to prevent targeted violence such as school shootings, workplace shootings, stalking, and assassination (Meloy et al., 2011). The threat assessment process consists of four components: (a) identifying (or receiving a report about) a person or situation that may pose a threat of violence; (b) gathering more information about that person or situation from multiple sources; (c) evaluating whether the person or situation poses a threat of violence to others, to self, or possibly to others *and* self; and (d) if needed, developing and implementing an individualized plan to reduce any threat posed (Deisinger, Randazzo, O'Neill, & Savage, 2008; Randazzo & Plummer, 2009).

The assessor or assessment team makes an evaluation by first answering several analytical questions about the person's ideas, plans, and capacity to do harm to a particular target, and then using that information to determine whether the person poses a threat — in other words, to determine if that person is thinking about and/or planning to harm the intended target. The threat assessment process is widely used to prevent violence and widely recommended because it is a deductive process: It focuses on facts — the behavior and communications of the person in question — and what conclusions those facts lead to, rather than focusing on whether the person in question matches any sort of "profile."

BEST PRACTICES IN CAMPUS THREAT ASSESSMENT

The ANSI-approved American national standard for colleges and universities identifies a few resources that institutions can look to for developing and operating a threat assessment program on campus (ASME, 2010). These resources detail the current best practices in campus threat assessment (see Deisinger et al., 2008; Randazzo & Plummer, 2009). Specifically, these resources emphasize that campus threat assessment is best accomplished by a *multidisciplinary team* with membership that represents a cross-section of offices, departments, and services across the institution. Multidisciplinary membership should include representatives from the following departments: student affairs (for contact with the student and with the student's family where necessary, to coordinate interaction with residential living and/or student conduct processes, etc.); campus safety (to assist with investigations, coordinate with local law enforcement, advise on need for no-contact orders or restraining orders, etc.); academic affairs (to access information regarding classroom performance and conduct, assist with accommodations, manage interactions with faculty members, etc.); campus ministry (to facilitate students' access to support

162

options, help monitor students' progress, and help facilitate reports of concern from campus ministers); counseling center or other mental health professional (to help facilitate students' access to and use of mental health support on or off campus, facilitate use of medical leaves of absence, and help the team understand what certain diagnoses or treatments mean and what to expect if there is medication non-compliance); and ad hoc members (the team can include representatives from specific departments, such as veterans services or international programs, as particular cases may warrant).

With respect to involving campus ministers in the threat assessment process, it is important to remember that although campus ministers may have private conversations with students and others on campus, they are typically not bound by confidentiality in the same way that priests or mental health professionals are. If campus ministers become aware of behavior or situations that raise concern about safety to individuals or to campus generally, they should be encouraged and empowered to share those concerns with the appropriate entities, such as a threat assessment team.

> "Campus threat assessment is best accomplished by a multidisciplinary team with membership that represents a cross-section of offices, departments, and services across the institution."

Once there is a threat assessment team, the team should have the authority to engage in efforts to identify, investigate, evaluate, and manage threatening and potentially dangerous behaviors on campus. The team should adopt a clear *mission statement* to define the scope of situations they will handle, including whether they will address behaviors of concern from current and former employees, visitors, and external threats — as well as threats from students (Deisinger et al., 2008). Some threat assessment teams handle situations in which there is concern about potential harm to others or to self and others; other threat assessment teams have a broader scope that includes situations in which there is concern about potential self-harm (but no concern about potential harm to others). Part of defining a team's scope is determining whether the threat assessment team will handle situations in which the only concern is about potential self-harm — and if not, where those cases should be referred so they don't get overlooked.

Further, the team should be trained in *threat assessment procedures* and instructed by qualified trainers with verified experience in the field of threat assessment. The team should also adopt some *operating guidelines*, based upon their training, to help guide how the team addresses a case from start to finish. Catholic college and universities should take care in selecting training for their threat assessment team. Campus security has become big business, with numerous vendors (including threat assessment trainers) claiming expertise they may not necessarily have. We recommend Catholic colleges and universities request recommendations from peer institutions that have received high-quality threat assessment training, and then conduct their own due diligence on those vendors. We also recommend asking vendors specific questions to vet their threat assessment expertise, as detailed in Randazzo and Deisinger's article on the issue (2015).

Finally, the team should identify and seek help accessing all available *intervention resources* for cases where they need to manage or reduce a threat. These resources often include counseling and other support services for students and employees (on campus or in the community), campus ministry resources, fair grievance procedures, disability services, career services, veterans' services, and liaison with local law enforcement. Other resources can include off-campus pastoral counseling, financial or credit counseling, and access to community resources such as domestic violence shelters or child protective services, among other resources.

THREAT ASSESSMENT IN CATHOLIC COLLEGES AND UNIVERSITIES

Catholic colleges and universities, in which guiding missions may include approaching people with compassion and providing care for the whole person, can be especially adept at providing support to those who may feel desperate or who have lost hope. This is true even when the institution may also need to administer some form of punishment to address the threatening behavior. Because of this, Catholic colleges and universities are particularly well-suited for developing and operating high-quality campus threat assessment programs. Empirical research on targeted violence in educational settings and in the workplace has shown that those who have engaged in targeted school, campus, or workplace violence have typically done so when they were at a point of personal desperation and saw few or no options left to solve their problems except through violence (Vossekuil et al., 2000). In order to prevent targeted violence, threat assessment team members may need to connect someone who is feeling desperate (and considering violence as a possible solution to their problems) with access to support and other resources to solve those problems through non-violent means.

Campus threat assessment programs work particularly well when they can provide both support and boundaries to a person whose behavior has raised concern. Catholic colleges and universities that can provide such support, as well as establish clear behavioral expectations and ideals, are often particularly well-suited to implement an effective threat assessment program. As institutions that are guided by compassion and focused on helping students (and others on campus) develop character, Catholic colleges and universities already embody some of the core principles that allow for threat assessment to work well.

CONCLUSION

The field of behavioral threat assessment and threat management has evolved from a process used solely by federal law enforcement to a multidisciplinary effort used widely in schools, colleges, workplaces, and other venues to evaluate threats and prevent intended violence. Catholic colleges and universities can ensure they develop and operate high-quality threat assessment programs by establishing a team, securing threat assessment training from qualified instructors, following procedural guidelines, and accessing necessary support and intervention resources. When accomplished within a campus climate that promotes compassion and care for the whole person, Catholic colleges and universities can prevent violence, help those who may be feeling desperate or hopeless, and enhance overall campus safety.

Marisa R. Randazzo is director of threat assessment at Georgetown University in Washington, DC.

REFERENCES

ASME Innovative Technologies Institute, LLC (2010). *A Risk Analysis Standard for Natural and Man-made Hazards to Higher Education Institutions.* Washington, DC: Author.

Deisinger, G., Randazzo, M., O'Neill, D., & Savage, J. (2008). *The Handbook for Campus Threat Assessment & Management Teams.* Boston: Applied Risk Management, LLC.

Dunkle, J., Silverstein, Z., & Warner S. (2008). "Managing Violent and Other Troubling Students: The Role of Threat Assessment Teams on Campus." *Journal of College and University Law* 34, 585-636.

International Association of Campus Law Enforcement Administrators (IACLEA) (2008). *Overview of the Virginia Tech Tragedy and Implications for Campus Safety: The IACLEA Blueprint for Safer Campuses.* West Hartford, CT: IACLEA.

Meloy, J.R., Hoffman, J., Guldimann, A., & James, D. (2011). "The Role of Warning Behaviors in Threat Assessment: An Exploration and Suggested Typology." *Behavioral Sciences and the Law,* doi:10.1002/bsl.

Randazzo, M. & Deisinger, G. (October 29, 2015). *How to Find a Good Threat Assessment Consultant: 5 Questions to Ask Before You Hire.* Available at http://www. sigmatma.com/how-to-find-a-good-threat-assessment-consultant-5-questions-to-ask-before-you-hire/.

Randazzo, M. & Plummer, E. (2009). *Implementing Behavioral Threat Assessment on Campus: A Virginia Tech Demonstration Project.* Blacksburg, VA: Virginia Tech University Press.

Vossekuil, B., Fein, R., Reddy, M., Borum, R., & Modzeleski, W. (2002). T*he Final Report and Findings of the Safe School Initiative: Implications for the Prevention of School Attacks in the United States.* Washington, DC: U.S. Department of Education and U.S. Secret Service.

PRINCIPLE SIX

Invites and accompanies students into the life of the Catholic Church through prayer, liturgy, sacraments, and spiritual direction.

CHAPTER 29 Richly, Deeply Supporting the Spiritual   **169**
Development of All

Julie Donovan Massey, St. Norbert College

CHAPTER 30 The Death of a Student: Lessons from a   **173**
Catholic Campus

Rev. Jay Fostner, OPraem, St. Norbert College

CHAPTER 29

Richly, Deeply Supporting the Spiritual Development of All

Julie Donovan Massey

St. Norbert College is a residential, liberal arts college of about 2,200 undergraduate students. We pride ourselves in being the only Catholic and Norbertine institution of higher education in the world. Located in De Pere, Wisconsin, we draw students primarily from Wisconsin, the Chicago area, and the upper Midwest. We capture a profile of each incoming class via the CIRP survey, from UCLA's Higher Education Research Institute, which students complete during orientation. Thus, each year, we know the profile of the religious affiliations our students *claim*. In some cases, those answers might come as a surprise to their parents or family members: "What do you mean 'none,' son? You are Catholic!" In other cases, the claim on the part of the student might not be deeply held: "I guess I'm Lutheran."

We know from these data that our student body is about 50–55 percent Roman Catholic; about 30–35 percent Christian of other traditions and backgrounds; and about 10–15 percent a mix of other world religions and no religious tradition, the latter being the far greater segment. With this context in mind, we will explore three areas of work from Principle Six of *Principles of Good Practice for Student Affairs at Catholic Colleges and Universities*, including ministering to Catholic students on our Catholic campuses, inviting all students to engage our Catholic tradition, and cultivating an environment of rich mentoring.

MINISTERING TO CATHOLIC STUDENTS ON OUR CATHOLIC CAMPUSES

Students attending Catholic institutions should find rich opportunities for prayer, vibrant attention to the sacramental life of the Church, and plentiful avenues to be encouraged in their spiritual growth. Common to Catholic campuses across the country are student-focused liturgies, sometimes in church or chapel spaces, sometimes in residence halls and other common areas. Here students assume greater responsibility for the sacramental life of the Church. Many of our students arrive having attended Mass only as often as their family required. Most have been passive participants and some likely actively resisted. Vibrant campus liturgies do not win over all Catholic students, but common is the story of a student who first joins a church choir or offers to lector during their college years. Because campus liturgies are often well-done and in tune with the life and needs of college students, it is on our campuses that many young people first experience Church as something of which they are a needed part.

Beyond sacramental offerings, our campus provides students opportunities to dive more deeply into the Catholic tradition. Certainly, this happens in required courses in theology and philosophy. But it also happens through such offerings as Kairos retreat experiences and through a weekly dialogue group called Donum Ipsum ("the gift itself") that delves into the richness of the Catholic tradition. Kairos retreats (a college adaptation of a proven high school model) and Donum Ipsum are unapologetically rooted in Catholic sacrament, belief, and practice. Open to anyone who wishes to participate, Kairos includes Catholic elements such as Adoration, Reconciliation, and Eucharist. Donum Ipsum includes reflection on the life of a saint and dialogue about various topics of interest to students. These programs serve as opportunities for students to explore their faith questions and convictions.

INVITING ALL STUDENTS TO ENGAGE OUR CATHOLIC TRADITION

If our Catholic institutions do not help all students better understand and appreciate the Roman Catholic tradition *and* deepen their own faith or spiritual commitments, we are failing in our mission. Students who come to us as Lutheran, Methodist, Muslim, non-denominational, agnostic, or from some other spiritual or faith grounding should graduate our institutions with a better understanding of the Catholic tradition. Again, some of this is gained in their coursework, as it should be. But, how can student affairs professionals and campus ministry staff contribute in the co-curricular part of the college experience?

On our campus, students encounter the Catholic tradition at the beginning of summer orientation, which starts in church and is steeped in prayer. In these first moments together, students and their families are introduced to members of the ministry and student development staffs; they hear about our grounding in the Catholic, Norbertine, and liberal arts traditions. The new students are blessed by their student mentors and their families. And the families themselves are blessed in recognition of this transitional moment in their family life.

An area St. Norbert College has focused on more deliberately in recent years is the need to foster contemplative practices. While we know our students are active, often overly so, the powerful message they need is a proclamation of the value of contemplative practices. Of course, the sacramental life of the Church is one place our students can find space for contemplation. Beyond that, we have offered models of time set apart. For a number of years, we held Sacred Hour from 10:00 a.m. to

11:00 a.m. on Wednesdays. People were asked to refrain from busy-ness as usual and spend time attending a weekly prayer service or listening to a faculty or staff member give an inspirational talk in the spirit of a Last Lecture. With the adoption of a new course schedule, our practice transitioned into a brief Morning Prayer service offered three mornings per week at 8:05 a.m. On Mondays and Wednesdays, the focus is on the scripture of the day with quiet reflection or a brief sermon. On Fridays, contemplative prayer is offered. Beyond Morning Prayer, we have offered centering prayer prior to common exam times, and one Norbertine priest gathers with the football team for a time of guided meditation before home games. In addition, we have deliberately built space for contemplation and have made a geographical commitment to the value of contemplation.

> "What is essential is an attitude of care and responsiveness for students drawn to our Catholic institutions and rooted in various expressions of faith."

Our ministry staff also works to meet the faith needs of students rooted in other Christian traditions or world religions. Our endeavors to attend to all our students have resulted in: creating a Spiritual Connections page on our website to connect students to faculty and staff from diverse backgrounds; offering a monthly worship service for Protestant students; and bringing onto our ministry staff a part-time Protestant minister. Such efforts signal to students and their families that our mission-based commitment to the spiritual development of our students exists for *all* students. What is essential is an attitude of care and responsiveness for students drawn to our Catholic institutions and rooted in various expressions of faith.

CULTIVATING AN ENVIRONMENT OF RICH MENTORING

There are two ways in particular that we have cultivated faculty and staff to help support the spiritual development of our students. The first is through the work of our vocation program, and the second is our focus on the Catholic Intellectual Tradition. In 2000, we were fortunate to have received nearly two million dollars from the Lilly Endowment, Inc. Over the years, St. Norbert College developed a significant program with elements including reading groups, workshops, retreats, and study groups for faculty and staff around the topic of vocation. We created a campus culture in which a sense of vocation is palpable. Survey data, program participation, and anecdotal evidence all point to the fact that our students are leaving campus with a deep sense that they are called to serve the needs of the world. (While the grant that supported us is no longer available, interested schools should explore membership in the Council of Independent College's Network for Vocation in Undergraduate Education [NetVUE] for both intellectual resources and access to smaller grants.)

Secondly, our ministry and mission areas have collaborated to provide opportunities for faculty and staff to directly engage the Catholic Intellectual Tradition. Whether through speakers on campus, the new faculty orientation program, Heritage Week offerings, or our Catholic Intellectual Tradition series, our colleagues have a chance to explore questions and deepen their understanding of this tradition. The more a diverse group of faculty and staff explores our institutional faith commitments, the better we can walk with all our students in their spiritual development.

At St. Norbert College, our ministry staff and our mission officers work together seamlessly. The ministry staff provides opportunities for students and oversees vocation efforts aimed at colleagues. Our mission officer has led efforts related to policy and practices that support the college's mission. In many cases, the two areas have collaborated in leadership — whether on our Heritage Days celebration, our Catholic Intellectual Tradition series, or work on hiring for mission. We see that the work of inviting students into rich engagement with the Catholic tradition is best achieved when those charged with mission responsibility and those overseeing ministry efforts are regularly in dialogue, supporting efforts that complement each other, and collaborating where it makes sense. In doing so, they can foster a campus experience that offers a vibrant face of the Catholic tradition to all who come.

Julie Donovan Massey is associate vice president for mission and student affairs at St. Norbert College in De Pere, Wisconsin.

CHAPTER 30

The Death of a Student: Lessons from a Catholic Campus

Jay Fostner, OPraem

We all have memories that stay with us forever. One of mine happened on a Sunday night, about ten years ago. Two of our female students had lost their lives in a traffic accident. I had just tracked down one of the girl's boyfriend to break the terrible news. After that difficult conversation, I headed off to another residence hall to notify the other girl's roommates. As I approached the door to her room, I overheard a young woman inside, a roommate, talking on her cell with her mother. "She's not answering her phone; she should be here by now. Something is wrong." I knocked. When the student opened the door and saw me standing there, I did not have to say a word; her fears were confirmed.

A decade ago, St. Norbert College experienced ten student deaths in just three years — well above the statistical average for a campus our size, about 2,100 students. Those experiences provided some sense of what worked, which issues caught us off guard, how we can support the process of human healing, and how the changing landscape of Catholic higher education might mean doing things differently. Sadly, we have had more occasions, including one while writing this chapter, to apply what we learned. Our experience has taught us two important lessons to remember.

First, no advice will work for every situation. Like all trauma, the event, the initial reaction, and how healing happens are different for every person and every community, and with every death. While developing protocols is important, at least to the point of knowing whom to call and having some initial ideas of response, in the end, what students and the community will need must be monitored constantly. What works for one situation might not work in another. Flexibility is essential.

Second, the greatest gift we have is that we work and minister on a Catholic campus. That fact gives us freedom that cannot be found on campuses that are not faith-based. Crises and death naturally result in questions and confusion. Our Catholic faith offers a theology of hope, rituals of healing, and the belief in a God who stays with us, even during the darkest of hours.

LESSON ONE: BE THE FIRST TO CALL

As campuses are physically compact and emotionally connected communities, news of any kind tends to spread quickly. Twice I have been on the phone with a parent of a student who just passed away, when tearful friends and neighbors suddenly showed up to offer condolences. Both sets of parents later thanked me that I had reached them first. I have often imagined what a shock it would have been to learn about the death of a child from a neighbor, who had no details or real information to offer, no matter how well intended the neighbor's action.

LESSON TWO: PRAY IMMEDIATELY

It does not matter whether one is Catholic, Protestant, Jewish, Muslim, or of no religion at all. Human beings, in time of tragedy, need to gather for support and understanding. We always offered the opportunity for the community to gather in prayer within hours of learning about the death of a student, especially when the student died on campus. Once, we sent a simple e-mail at 2:00 a.m. letting the campus know about a death and that there would be a prayer service at 3:00 a.m. The result was a church overflowing with community members.

The prayer service was not carefully planned, and precision was not necessary. What the community wanted most was to gather. So we quickly wrote an opening prayer, found a scripture reading, wrote some prayers of petition, and closed with an "Our Father." Near the conclusion of the service, we gave the campus community resources about grieving, and information about where to find support and how we would keep the community informed. At this point, we could not tell the community the details of what had happened, but we took the time to share enough information that rumors were squelched. By correcting inaccurate information, additional trauma was reduced.

Since then, we have developed an outline for these prayer experiences, including a list of potential scripture passages, songs, and prayers that can be used when a young person dies. But we have not designed a complete prototype. We found that the community, almost instantaneously, responded to each death differently. One of the great gifts in working on a Catholic campus is the rich treasury of religious language that can be used during difficult times. The entire campus community, Catholic or not, readily accepts the language and rituals as part of the institution's fabric and identity.

We considered celebrating Mass instead of having a prayer service when the death of a student was initially announced. We found a prayer service worked well. It was not because Mass can be exclusionary. In times of crisis, Catholics and non-Catholics alike will gather for Mass. But our experience suggests that students, at least immediately after learning about the death of a friend, need something less formal than a Mass. When the shock of losing a student colleague is still sinking in, having to respond with a simple phrase like, "And with your Spirit," or knowing when to stand or kneel, can feel overwhelming.

LESSON THREE: WHO TAKES THE LEAD?

While detailed protocols may not be appropriate, there are a few things that should be decided before a crisis occurs. It is during times like these that campus staff can inadvertently "step on one another." Before a crisis occurs, decide who initially takes the lead and who will be responsible for various activities. This is a time when student affairs and campus ministry need to be on the same page.

LESSON FOUR: REMEMBER TO TAKE TIME

Naturally, we want to help our campus communities move through the pain as quickly as possible. But working against human nature can be a mistake. It takes time to work through our immediate reaction to loss. And as student affairs professionals, we need to help our community remember that *time* is an important step in the grieving process.

LESSON FIVE: THE IMPORTANCE OF HONESTY

Student affairs personnel can be put in awkward, or even angry, situations when confronted with a student crisis or death. Community members want to know what has happened. When the cause of death is sensitive — in the case of a suicide, for instance — it may be difficult for staff to tell the entire story. In one such instance, moments after a student's death, we communicated to the campus that, out of respect for the family, we were not able to release details, but that we would provide more information in the future. This helped the community have a respectful context in which to understand the lack of immediate information available. We have often found that after a few days, but before the wake and funeral, a family is willing to give permission to "tell the whole story."

In this case, the family gave us permission to do so. We carefully wrote an e-mail to the campus, letting friends, faculty, and staff know the details of what had happened. This proved healing, not only for the community, but for the family as well. It removed the pressure of trying to hide facts. More importantly, we found that once the community was aware of the circumstances, the family was showered with even greater compassion, love, and support.

LESSON SIX: THE MINISTRY OF PRESENCE

I am often asked what is the best thing to say to family and friends who have just lost a loved one. "No words will really help," I tell them, "but your presence will mean everything."

Being present is an obvious way to promote healing, but there are some subtle takeaways that should be considered. First, during the initial phone call, give the family one person they can contact with any questions or requests. Having too many people from the university contact the family, or expecting the family to figure out whom to contact, is a mistake.

Do everything possible to make sure the campus community is present at services for those families who have an open funeral and later, offer a campus memorial service. At that time, if the family is Catholic, we suggest celebrating the Eucharist. Further, we have found one of the *most powerful moments in the grieving process* to be when a family member speaks at the memorial service. These are potent moments, moments that stay with community members, especially students, indefinitely.

Stay in touch with the family. While some things are obvious, such as sending a Christmas card or planting a memorial tree, one thing that we initiated was a posthumous degree for any student who had junior or senior standing. During the graduation ceremony, after all other students received their degrees, we lit a candle and invited family members up to receive a diploma. Be ready; there will not be a dry eye in the audience.

CONCLUSION

If you experience the crisis of a student death, it *will* be a difficult time. Our experience confirms that grieving and healing are processes and there is no one right way to respond. Have some initial protocols, but remain flexible and pull together relevant staff to discuss the six lessons described here. While painful, we believe in a God who promises abounding mercy and unconditional love.

Rev. Jay Fostner, OPraem, is vice president for mission and student affairs and assistant professor of psychology at St. Norbert College in De Pere, Wisconsin.

PRINCIPLE SEVEN

Seeks dialogue among religious traditions and with contemporary culture to clarify beliefs and to foster mutual understanding in the midst of tensions and ambiguities.

CHAPTER 31   Creating an Interfaith Culture at a Catholic   **179**
University and Meeting the Spiritual and
Religious Needs of All Students

*Lisa R. Reiter, Loyola University Chicago,
and Crystal Caruana Sullivan, University of
Dayton*

CHAPTER 32   Praying Together: Celebrating Ritual in   **185**
Inclusive Communities

*Michael Lovette-Colyer, University of
San Diego*

CHAPTER 31

Creating an Interfaith Culture at a Catholic University and Meeting the Spiritual and Religious Needs of All Students

Lisa R. Reiter and Crystal Caruana Sullivan

Catholic universities foster a vibrant interfaith culture because, by their nature, they value hospitality, religious literacy, and human dignity. The value of hospitality has its origin in the book of Genesis 18:1-15, when Abraham and Sarah welcome three strangers, greeting them, offering them water to bathe and succulent roast meat and fresh baked bread to eat. The strangers bring good news, announcing that Sarah will bear a son. This exchange is marked by openness, mutuality, and self-giving. With it taking place over a meal, it stands in prophetic relationship to the Eucharistic and table fellowship of Jesus. The value of hospitality is embodied in Catholic universities when they welcome students of diverse religious identities.

In a world polarized by religious fundamentalism and ignorance, Catholic universities have a responsibility to educate students for religious literacy with the aspiration of strengthening relationships among people of different religious traditions. Many of the conflicts that afflict communities around the world originate from religious fundamentalism, which denigrates those of another faith tradition. In today's global workplace, students need religious literacy to understand the beliefs and values of their co-workers and clients.

Respect for human dignity is a fundamental teaching of Catholicism. Catholic universities embody this value by educating students holistically, mind, body, and spirit.

Ex corde Ecclesia consistently emphasizes that "when the academic community includes members of other Churches, ecclesial communities or religions, their initiatives for reflection and prayer in accordance with their own beliefs are to be respected" (39). In *Nostra Aetate*, the Church affirms the truths and sacredness of precepts and teachings of non-Christian religions. *The Principles of Good Practice for Student Affairs in Catholic Colleges and Universities* affirms this commitment to religious diversity by dedicating Principle Seven to interfaith dialogue and understanding. This interfaith work at Catholic colleges and universities is accomplished through collaborative efforts including academic units, student affairs, campus ministry, dining services, facilities, campus recreation, and more. These collaborative efforts have established a range of best practices.

BEST PRACTICES

Examining the religious demographics of the student population helps student affairs and campus ministry offices partner to advocate for needed resources. Understanding the demographics of the student body will be invaluable to those who make decisions regarding resources and services for religiously diverse students.

In the recruitment process for prospective students, the offices that are responsible for admissions and orientation need to be attentive to the institution's Catholic identity. Admissions counselors, who are comfortable explaining the Catholic university's commitment to fostering the religious and spiritual development of all students, can help allay the fears of parents that their children will be converted to Catholicism against their will and that the institution has supports in place for students of other faith traditions.

The university should determine an office to take leadership for coordinating interfaith activities. While campus ministry is often tasked with this leadership, accommodating the religious needs of students requires coordination among a variety of campus offices. For example, dining services should be attentive to halal or kosher requirements for Muslim or Jewish students, as they would be for Catholic Lenten observances. The provost's office should be familiar with religious high holy days and educate faculty regarding potential student requests for absences or deadline extensions. Campus recreation services may be called upon to provide gender-specific exercise classes to accommodate Muslim women, who would never attend a co-ed class.

During orientation and welcome week, many Catholic universities have a custom of celebrating Mass for the whole academic community. Complementary to the opening Mass, activities that welcome religiously diverse students should be offered, including opportunities to pray with one's faith community or in an interfaith setting. Open houses and fairs, whereby students may learn about programs and prayer sponsored by their faith community, help foster community and strengthen religious identity.

A particularly important issue of interfaith hospitality is access to sacred space. Designated spaces, while requiring significant resources, facilitate strong identities among students of certain traditions. Shared spaces are more challenging to design, but their presence contributes to attitudes of interfaith cooperation on campus.

A variety of factors should be taken into consideration when planning for new sacred space. Planners, including students who will use the space, should identify how sacred space will be used and whether it serves believers from one tradition or is shared by many. Beauty is a factor that must be considered, especially given the temptation to set aside "empty rooms" as sacred spaces. With careful consideration and some investment in familiar devotional aids (prayer beads, sacred texts, etc.), lighting, color, texture, and the addition of simple architectural features, spaces can be designed that are worthy of use by people of a variety of traditions.

> "Multi-faith prayer honors the traditions of many by weaving resources and ritual elements from a variety of traditions into a common prayer experience."

Modeling and developing the capacity for multi-faith prayer is also of value on Catholic campuses. Multi-faith prayer honors the traditions of many by weaving resources and ritual elements from a variety of traditions into a common prayer experience. Such an experience has elements that are recognizable to people from disparate traditions (e.g., combined use of sacred readings, varied use of candles, water, incense, music, participants from various perspectives, languages, etc.). Generally, this is preferable to generic prayer that avoids religiously specific names and titles for God or any confessional language. One principle to keep in mind with multi-faith prayer is to avoid inviting the assembly to make confessional statements through choral readings or responses. In this way, participants can witness and be inspired by the combination of prayer elements from a variety of traditions, but are not required to assent to specific belief statements as they participate.

MODELS OF INTERFAITH MINISTRY

Three ministry models for supporting religious diversity have emerged on Catholic campuses. These include the student organization model, the interfaith chaplain model, and the dedicated chaplain model. Determining which model is best is a campus-specific process that depends on mission, student demographics, and resources.

In the *student organization model,* student-led organizations for faith traditions represented on campus are encouraged. Through these, students emerge as leaders, advocate for their own needs, offer opportunities for religiously specific formation, and provide opportunities for campus education and social engagement. As contributors to the culture of faith expression on campus, organizations should have a relationship with campus ministry through advising, liaison relationships, or interfaith councils. The student organization model is most successful when a critical mass of interested students exists from a particular tradition. Without this, leadership is difficult to maintain and organizations easily flounder.

In the *interfaith chaplain model,* a single campus minister serves as a resource for building interfaith cooperation on campus. The interfaith chaplain is knowledgeable about a wide range of religious traditions, able to build relationships with off-campus resources, offers opportunities for religious literacy development among the entire campus community, and serves as a spiritual resource for a variety of students. A variation on the interfaith chaplain model is the interfaith organization. Here, students from a variety of traditions form one unified ministry to develop interfaith relationships and provide opportunities for religious literacy development. These organizations have a strong capacity to form student leaders with interfaith competencies and leadership skills. The interfaith model can be very successful, especially on campuses whose religious diversity is small or where stronger cooperation among students of a variety of religious traditions is valued. On the other hand, the interfaith chaplain may lack the capacity to provide denomination-specific resources when students need them. Students and chaplains may often need to rely on off-campus support.

In the *dedicated chaplain model,* the campus ministry staff represents the religious demographics of the campus community. For example, a rabbi, imam, swami, or other Christian minister might serve alongside campus ministers who specialize in serving the more general student body. Campuses that adopt this model typically have a critical mass of students from one or more religious traditions. Campuses with dedicated chaplains can focus specifically on faith formation for students from a variety of traditions, in the same way they might for Catholic students. The presence of dedicated chaplains also greatly enhances the interfaith character of the ministry staff and increases the capacity of the campus ministry team to cultivate leaders from all faith traditions who are competent in interfaith leadership. A major consideration for the dedicated chaplain model is that it requires significant financial resources and administrative oversight to sustain and be successful.

Incorporating some or all of these best practices will help Catholic universities continue to support students' holistic development and foster environments that are rich in interfaith dialogue and understanding. In doing so, they prepare graduates who will navigate the religiously diverse landscape with competence and sensitivity.

Lisa R. Reiter is the director of campus ministry at Loyola Chicago University in Chicago, Illinois. Crystal Caruana Sullivan is director of campus ministry at the University of Dayton in Dayton, Ohio.

CHAPTER 32

Praying Together:
Celebrating Ritual in Inclusive Communities

Michael Lovette-Colyer

Sacramentality — seeing the extraordinary in the ordinary, the infinite in the finite, the divine in the human — is one of the most distinctive elements of the Catholic tradition. This way of viewing the world, often described as the Catholic imagination, was perhaps best expressed by the great nineteenth century Jesuit poet Gerard Manley Hopkins (1953) who wrote, "The world is charged with the grandeur of God" (p. 27). Reflecting on what he terms the sacramental principle, theologian Michael Himes (2004) suggested the "whole Catholic tradition can be thought of as a training in becoming sacramental beholders" (p. 14). In other words, cultivating an increasing ability to recognize the presence of God in each and every aspect of life is central to Catholicism, as well as to Catholic higher education.

Primarily, this way of seeing is expressed and practiced on Catholic campuses through annual rituals such as an opening Mass, commissioning of resident assistants and other student leaders, blessing of athletic jerseys, various award ceremonies and honors convocations, and the Baccalaureate Mass. These special events function to remind the community that God is always present and active in its midst, witnessing to the graced reality of campus life every day of the year.

In light of the growing diversity of Catholic colleges and universities, as well as the "rise of the none's" — the dramatic increase in college-aged Americans who do not identify with a religious tradition (Pew Center for Religion, 2012) — the manner in which these rituals are celebrated needs thoughtful consideration. Before offering some suggestions on how best to accomplish this, we will consider the reality of rituals in general and the role they play in our lives. After situating rituals in that context, we will then consider the best way to celebrate them on the contemporary Catholic campus.

RITUAL

The word *ritual* derives from the Latin *ritualis*, which refers to the proven way of doing something. In general, a ritual can be thought of as a well-established sequence, typically involving specific words, gestures, and objects, conducted in a specially designated location. Rituals can be religious, but they also exist on the individual, family, and university levels. For example, an individual ritual might revolve around a cup of coffee in the morning or taking the dog out for a walk after work. Families with young children have well-established evening rituals involving bath, books, and bedtime. University life is full of rituals; no moment on campus is more ritualized than the weekend when new students arrive to be welcomed into the academic community. All campuses have well-established sequences, involving specific words, gestures, and objects, as well as specially designed places for this important moment.

A Catholic appreciation of ritual centers on the way in which they provide punctuation, allowing us to make meaning out of the run-on sentences and tangled paragraphs of our often frenetic, fragmented lives. Rituals provide the time and space necessary for the reflection out of which wisdom can emerge. They operationalize the principle of sacramentality, allowing us to see the extraordinary in the ordinary, the infinite in the finite, the divine in the human.

This expansive way of thinking about rituals is essential to realizing that rituals are not exclusively for Catholics, or Buddhists, Hindus, Jews, Muslims, or other people of faith. Instead, rituals are human activities that play important roles in our lives — including in our personal lives, in our families, and in our colleges and universities. Having emphasized the fundamentally human nature of rituals, we now turn to consider ways they can be effectively and inclusively celebrated in contemporary, religiously diverse Catholic colleges and universities.

CELEBRATING RITUALS WELL

In light of the evolving religious landscape on our campuses, there is no one right way to arrange and celebrate campus rituals. The particular history, charism — from the Greek term charisma, meaning a gift from the Holy Spirit which empowers an individual or a community "to do ordinary things extraordinarily well" and sometimes enables "ordinary people to do extraordinary things" (Haughey, 1999, p. 1) — traditions, cultural make-up, and geography of each school ought to influence the rituals sponsored. Nevertheless, three foundational guidelines may help Catholic colleges and universities discern how best to offer rituals that speak to the wide range of students, faculty, and staff they serve.

Guideline One: Eucharist Is Central to Catholic Identity

As the "source and summit of Christian life" (*Lumen Gentium*, 11), graceful, captivating Eucharistic celebrations should hold a privileged place in the rhythm of the Catholic campus. A Catholic university, to be vibrantly Catholic, needs to be grounded in and connected to the Eucharist (*Ex corde Ecclesiae*, 39). The tradition of beginning the year with a university-wide Eucharist and ending with the Baccalaureate Mass is a best practice. However, campuses need to ensure that all members of the community — from all faith backgrounds — are enthusiastically invited to attend. Such invitations ought to emphasize the unique opportunity these rituals provide to join together as one community to give thanks to God for the blessings afforded by higher education.

> "Provide one campus-wide experience each year that reflects the Catholic appreciation for diverse faith traditions."

In addition to well-crafted invitations, hospitality at Eucharistic rituals is critical. When people arrive, they should be greeted with sufficient warmth and joy to communicate the truth that each member of the community belongs at, and has a place in, the ritual. A carefully created worship aid is also essential; such a document will help attendees understand, feel comfortable during, and participate in the ritual. Finally, in order to make annual Eucharistic celebrations as meaningful as possible, the particular needs, intentions, and desires of the community should be thoughtfully woven into the prayers, musical selections, homily, and all other aspects of the Mass.

Guideline Two: Sponsor a Prominent Interfaith Prayer Service

The second guideline for celebrating campus rituals is to provide one campus-wide experience each year that reflects the Catholic appreciation for diverse faith traditions. The start of the second semester or winter quarter is a particularly opportune time to schedule such an interfaith prayer gathering, echoing the Mass held at the beginning of the fall term. Including an interfaith ritual in the rhythm of the academic year offers multiple benefits, including the opportunity to highlight a Catholic approach to diversity and inclusion (celebrating diversity because of our Catholicity, not despite it) as well as to educate the community about the richness and beauty of the world's religious traditions. While interfaith rituals offer many advantages, they also introduce several challenges. First among these is the imperative to avoid tokenism and cultural appropriation by ensuring that leaders and/or members of the various faith traditions lead the prayer service. A second challenge is structuring the ritual in a way that allows each faith to be adequately represented in the short time such an interfaith prayer service affords. Finally, without great care, interfaith rituals can become performances rather than shared moments of prayer. In light of these challenges, as well as the inherent complexity involved with bringing together faith traditions, it is recommended to charge a carefully selected committee to coordinate interfaith rituals.

Guideline Three: Ground Ordinary Academic Life in the Context of Faith

The third and final guideline for celebrating campus rituals is to weave moments of faith into the regular routines of the community's life. The profoundly human and universal reality of rituals can be highlighted, for example, by beginning campus meetings and ceremonies with a prayer (including from disparate faith traditions) or moments of silent stillness. Holidays and holy days in the world's religions (such as the start and end of Ramadan, the Jewish holy days of Yom Kippur and Rosh Hashanah, as well as Advent and Lent) should be recognized through campus e-mail announcements. Likewise, important cultural celebrations connected to religious traditions, such as Martin Luther King Jr. Day, the Feast of Our Lady of Guadalupe, and Kwanzaa can and should be acknowledged. Campuses can also promote more regular rituals such as weekly or daily Mass, Friday prayer, Seder meals, and penance services.

CONCLUSION

By consistently calling attention to the vital role of faith and by identifying particular moments when this role is most salient, Catholic colleges and universities can expand appreciation for and understanding of ritual. Along with the carefully planned and beautifully celebrated university-wide rituals, this enhanced appreciation has the power to spark the sacramental imagination that is at the heart of the Catholic tradition.

Michael Lovette-Colyer is assistant vice president and director of university ministry at the University of San Diego in San Diego, California.

REFERENCES

Haughey, J. C. (1999). "Charisms: An Ecclesiological Exploration," in D. Donnelly (Ed.) *Retrieving Charisms for the Twenty-First Century*. Collegeville, MN: Order of St. Benedict, Inc.

Himes, M. J. (2004). *The Mystery of Faith: An Introduction to Catholicism*. Cincinnati, OH: St. Anthony Messenger Press.

Hopkins, G. M. (1953). *Poems and Prose*. London: Penguin Press.

Pew Research Center. (2012). None's on the Rise. Retrieved from http://www.pewforum.org/2012/10/09/nones-on-the-rise/.

PRINCIPLE EIGHT

Assists students in discerning and responding to their vocations, understanding potential professional contributions, and choosing particular career directions.

CHAPTER 33 Mission-centric Recruitment   **191**

Edward P. Wright, Mount St. Mary's University

CHAPTER 34 The Manresa Program: Learning,   **197**
Meaning, Calling, and Career

Deborah Cady Melzer, Le Moyne College

CHAPTER 33

Mission-centric Recruitment

Edward P. Wright

"Be who God meant you to be and you will set the world on fire."
— Saint Catherine of Siena

To explore Catholic higher education admissions practices, this chapter will focus on the following themes: mission-centric recruitment strategies, vocational exploration, affordability and value, and ethical obligations. Effective admissions professionals articulate the value of Catholic higher education to prospective students and families, and Catholic institutions validate the views of families while guiding them away from outside pressures.

MISSION

Consider a typical admissions event scheduled for accepted students (yield program). As the family checks in, they see the above quote from Catherine of Siena on the wall and the parent stops to reflect. Mom knows; she is sold on the school. But the admissions officer prepares for the typical questions: How Catholic are you? Are you a "big C" or "little c" Catholic campus? Many staff from Catholic institutions are asked these questions; it is nothing new. This occasion has a happy ending. Mom is happy, because it is her favorite university.

Living the mission of educating students to be greater citizens of the Church and the world is a daunting task. Admissions officers begin that conversation with prospective students and families. They must relate how their institution lives these goals and supports each student through his or her journey. Students are encouraged to explore their vocations, to find the path God is calling them to follow. This path includes navigating academic, social, athletic, and co-curricular contributions. The Council for the Advancement of Standards in Higher Education lays out the general responsibility of every admissions professional, which includes knowing enough about each area to counsel their students (2009).

VOCATION EXPLORATION

Institutional mission statements are living documents that admissions officers rely on to steer recruitment strategies and messages. Grounded in these statements are the conversations admissions officers have with prospective families focused on the meaning and purpose of a Catholic higher education. Admissions officers must be comfortable explaining how their institution integrates beliefs, gifts, ambitions, and hopes within their academic and faith tradition. This tradition focuses on all students, including those from underserved populations and those with limited financial means. Families will begin to see the balance between achieving a college degree and the influence of a faith tradition. The balance an institution strikes will parallel the balance a student faces between his or her professional, personal, and relational commitments.

At a Catholic institution, opportunities exist to frame this balance within the conversation of vocation. Students are encouraged to choose an academic program that interests them and relates to their passions. Vocations are integrated into a student's personal and professional life. Students are urged to discern their passion and to live it in all aspects of their lives. Admissions officers can encourage these conversations early and often by guiding families to think beyond the college image commonly portrayed in the media. It is often easy for families to direct students to specific career paths in high school and encourage them to remain on them through graduate studies. Those outside the college setting may believe it will take longer to graduate, and be less affordable, if a student explores other academic fields.

VALUE AND AFFORDABILITY

Admissions officers must reframe the question of cost to one of value and affordability. Value becomes apparent as conversations on vocation, meaning, and purpose intersect with the affordability of Catholic higher education. Families are conditioned by peers and the media to seek the most affordable or lowest-cost education, leading to the least debt after graduation. Similarly, students are pushed to select professional programs that will lead to larger pay checks following graduation.

A family might appreciate the beauty of a campus, enjoy the tour, and find the student's desired major, only to stop when they see the cost of tuition ("sticker shock"). An admissions officer must be able to explain that the total cost of a student's education is not always born solely by the student or the family. Conversations shift to affordability. The ability of an admissions officer to navigate the world of financial aid is indispensable. If scholarships and grants are available, how are they promoted? Some institutions are transparent and state, "If you have X.XX GPA and XXXX

> "Any conversation about costs should immediately be followed by one of affordability and value."

SAT/ACT scores, then you are guaranteed this scholarship." Others will promote a discount rate: "If you have these qualifications, we will take XX% off tuition." A Catholic institution makes great headway when discussing the discount rates and "free money" options that make their school more affordable and attractive. Any conversation about costs should immediately be followed by one of affordability and value.

An admissions office relies on the mission of the institution to guide marketing and recruitment strategies, along with the admissions officer's ability to convey the worth of a Catholic education. Staff must be able to explain the mission and values of the Catholic institution, as well as offer examples of how they are authentic and alive in the experiences and education of its students. Those values are often centered on service, the common good, educating the whole person, honoring the dignity of each person, liberal arts formation, faith, and the spiritual development of students.

ETHICAL OBLIGATIONS

An ethical obligation exists between an admissions office and prospective families. This obligation to represent Catholic values in a positive and accurate way often is presented in marketing materials, recruitment events, and student/ staff conversations. At a Catholic institution, the focus should shift to recruiting, retaining, and graduating its students. Colorful photos of students in front of picturesque campus buildings, specific quotes to reinforce the literature, and even the presenter's comments all convey a specific institutional message. Admissions officers at Catholic institutions must be more critical of what they say and share with families. These materials, conversations, and presentations should reflect the mission of the institution, exude what the institution stands for, and demonstrate the experiences of the community members. This open and forthright approach will convince students and families to consider the institution as their next home.

Ethical obligations produce challenging conversations for admissions officers. It will be necessary for some families to look at other college options and they will need a professional to guide them. Not all students are prepared for college or have the academic achievement necessary to thrive. Some are better served by attending a community college, then transferring to a four-year institution. The most difficult conversations focus on affordability, when an officer realizes no amount of additional aid will make college a viable option. At a Catholic institution, it is the admissions officer's responsibility to point out that a particular family's debt may be greater than they are able to bear. There is an ethical obligation, one founded in the beliefs of Catholic Social Teaching and justice, to ensure the families served understand all options regarding affordability and debt management. If these conversations do not happen honestly during the application and decision cycle, the ability to gather finances for only one year will not serve the student's financial obligations during the following three years of college.

RESOURCES

There are useful documents worth reviewing on admissions programs and ethical standards. In a section of its standards on undergraduate admissions programs, the Council for the Advancement of Standards in Higher Education states, "The admissions professional must also have a firm understanding of the institution's mission, enrollment goals, fiscal priorities, and student and departmental needs" (2009). Most admissions professionals connect with colleagues through the National Association for College Admission Counseling (NACAC). NACAC's *Statement of Principles of Good Practice* outlines core values, conventions, and best practices. These statements speak to an admissions officer's ethical obligation to be fair and equitable when working with students by ensuring their access to the institutions in which they have the greatest interest. Admissions officers are counselors, recruiters, and enrollment professionals all at the same time (NACAC, 2013). In addition, the National Catholic College Admission Association provides resources for prospective students, counselors, and college admission professionals.

CONCLUSION

College admissions officers are called upon to be honest and reflective in practice. An admissions office must have a process in place to judge the effectiveness of its efforts. Evidence in the form of data collection and analysis is necessary. If data and survey tools do not exist, they need to be created and used moving forward. Asking tough questions of the students who choose your institution, and of those who choose to go elsewhere, is important. If an institution values vocational exploration, it must also be willing to explore its own practices and respond to what the data demonstrate. In the end, admissions professionals are the first to encourage students to shine brightly in the pursuit of the paths to which God is calling them.

Edward P. Wright is the associate director of admissions at Mount St. Mary's University in Emmitsburg, Maryland.

REFERENCES

Council for the Advancement of Standards in Higher Education. (2009). *CAS Self-assessment Guide for Admission Programs.* Washington, DC: CAS.

National Association for College Admission Counseling. (2013). *Statement of Principles of Good Practice.* Washington, DC: NACAC.

National Catholic College Admission Association. (2014). Retrieved from http://www.catholiccollegesonline.org/.

CHAPTER 34

The Manresa Program: Learning, Meaning, Calling, and Career

Deborah Cady Melzer

INTRODUCTION

Higher education is increasingly under pressure to provide students with the skills necessary to find employment. Families want their students to receive training in a specialty with experiences that distinguish each student, with the goal of immediate employment upon graduation. The growing cost of higher education has led to questioning "the value of the college degree and the career outcomes it historically promises" (Contomanolis et al., 2015, p. 23). The value of the liberal arts education is difficult to market in light of these expectations for colleges and universities to provide pre-professional academic experiences that result in job placement and high starting salaries.

In addition to providing the skills necessary to succeed in work, Catholic colleges and universities have promoted the values of service to others, deep reflection, and the value of a well lived life. Careers become more than simply a place of employment but instead, a vocation that transcends the boundaries of work and home to a more holistic sense of self. As Moore (2008) explains, "By definition a life work is deep-seated and emotional. A person will only feel connected to his life work if his (sic) job allows deep emotions, memory, and the love of doing something significant" (p. 42). Work is the deepest expression of our passions, talents, and contributions to our surrounding communities. Both the challenge and the call to Catholic colleges and universities is to provide our students with holistic experiences that prepare them for lives of meaning and purpose.

These external pressures, coupled with our mission to educate students for a life of meaning and service, led Le Moyne College to start *The Manresa Program: Integrating Learning, Meaning, Calling, and Career*. Manresa, the town where St. Ignatius wrote the spiritual exercises, became the inspiration for a four-year vocational discernment program. With generous support from the Council of Independent Colleges' Network for Vocation in Undergraduate Education (NetVUE) program, Le

Moyne College has been able to support a variety of pilot experiences and speakers to launch the Manresa program. This chapter describes the program and the ways in which Le Moyne has responded to the integration of a liberal arts education with pre-professional readiness grounded in our enduring values.

OVERVIEW OF THE PROGRAM

Manresa: Integrating Learning, Meaning, Calling, and Career is an intentional four-year program that engages students during each year of their college experience. The Manresa program meets students where they are in their vocational journey and allows them to deeply examine three questions: Who am I? What are my talents? Where do my talents best serve the world? As a developmental program, Manresa challenges students to reflect deeply on their own skills and values, while simultaneously engaging in professional and career development. The program integrates the students' experiences inside and outside the classroom by providing opportunities for rich conversation and deep reflection for personal, professional, and spiritual growth. A number of elements of the Manresa program connect classroom and co-curricular learning and these elements are organized around four themes: Become You, Values in Action, Think Forward, and Meaningful Success.

Become You

During the first year of college in Become You, students are given opportunities alongside mentors to engage in rich self-discovery. Students uncover their strengths, talents, and passions in order to understand who they can become. Through self-reflection and peer conversation, students begin to discover career and life paths that best fulfill their unique potentials. Tools such as the Myers Briggs Type Inventory, journaling, group exercises, vocational readings, and videos assist first-year students in owning their personal journeys by understanding their sense of self within a network of peers.

Values in Action

During the sophomore year of college, students explore Values in Action. The experience moves from the exploration of "me" to an understanding of the "we." Students in this program begin to explore the world around them and develop a deeper understanding of their own sense of responsibility to put their skills and talents to work for the greater good. Values inventories and social justice readings and materials prepare students for work in the local community through internships, job shadowing, and service learning. Service in the community becomes the cornerstone experience of this year, guided by mentor-facilitated reflection. This holistic approach complements the Ignatian pedagogy of experience, reflection, and action. As students understand and practice their values, they become empowered to be men and women for and with others and live the Jesuit value of *cura personalis,* care for the whole person.

Think Forward

The junior year of college is a critical time when students begin to Think Forward with further preparation for careers and callings. As students settle into a career path, they begin to deepen their co-curricular experiences with internships, study abroad, and academic research. The student mentoring experience becomes more individualized through intensive work with a faculty member or employer. During the Think Forward year, students affirm their talents and values through real-life experiences that challenge their perceptions of the world, the values they hold, and the meaning of their chosen calling. Their spiritual lives are deepened as they move from the dualistic perspective of seeing the world, toward the complexities of multiple perspectives to solve real-world problems.

Meaningful Success

Although the focus of senior year is life after graduation, students in year four, Meaningful Success, are challenged to view success as more than employment. They come to understand that success requires us to see life as the tireless pursuit of the best possible version of oneself. Although the outcomes of employment or graduate study are still desired, students leave the program more connected to their calling with greater passion and love. In this stage of the program, students are giving back through engagement with younger students exploring life questions. Catholic college missions allow for and often provide opportunities for each student to contribute to our communities. Seniors in Meaningful Success give back to the program as mentors to first- and second-year students, and thus model the richness of community life when engaged in deep reflection and conversation.

STRUCTURE OF THE CONVERSATION

The process of the Manresa program is as important as the content delivered. As Parks (2000) indicates, students are engaged in life questions around the self, other, the world, and faith, and best explore those questions in the context of mentoring friendships in community. During Manresa, students engage in 90-minute small group mentoring conversations over the course of a semester or year. In mentoring pairs, trained faculty, staff, and alumni facilitate in a similar method so that students learn a form of dialogue and reflection consistent with tools of discernment, which also aids in building trust and community.

Following 15–20 minutes of centering and initial check-in activities, the mentor group moves into the topic of the week. The topic is introduced by engaging in some type of activity. These activities can include personality inventories (done in advance, with results presented at meetings), letters from family and friends, values inventory, leadership maps, watching videos, short lectures, or readings. The topic is presented as a common experience that allows participants the opportunity to engage with material that sparks personal reflection and group discussion. The common experience is then followed up with journal questions that students individually write about, then share with a partner. The entire group re-engages in discussion and closes with a reflection, short reading, or prayer.

CONCLUSION

The Manresa program provides opportunities for students to integrate their college curricular and co-curricular experiences in order to grow personally, professionally, and spiritually while preparing for success in a rapidly changing world. Catholic colleges and universities are uniquely positioned to educate and prepare students for careers that are purposeful and meaningful, and the Manresa program is a model for such education. The *Manresa Program: Integrating Learning, Meaning, Calling, and Career* fulfills the distinctive intent of Catholic higher education: to prepare graduates for a life of meaning, purpose, and leadership in our global community.

Deborah Cady Melzer is the vice president for student development at Le Moyne College in Syracuse, New York.

REFERENCES

Contomanolis, E., Cruzvergara, C., Dey, F., Steinfeld, T., (2015). "The Future of Career Services Is Now." *NACE Journal* LXXVI (2), 23-28.

Moore, T. (2008). *A Life at Work: The Joy of Discovering What You Were Born to Do.* New York: Broadway Books.

Parks, S. (2000). *Big Questions, Worthy Dreams: Mentoring Young Adults in Their Search for Meaning, Purpose and Faith.* San Francisco: Harper.

Pope Francis. Address of Pope Francis to students and teachers from schools across Italy. May 10, 2014. Retrieved from http://w2.vatican.va/content/francesco/en/speeches/2014/may/documents/papa-francesco_20140510_mondo-della-scuola.html.

Made in the USA
San Bernardino, CA
22 November 2017